Presley
_____

From

Gran Gran &
_____
     Grandady

Date

4 • 20 • 19
_____

When
JESUS
Speaks to a
Girl's
Heart

When JESUS Speaks to a Girl's Heart

Janice Thompson

BARBOUR BOOKS
An Imprint of Barbour Publishing, Inc.

© 2017 by Barbour Publishing, Inc.

Print ISBN 978-1-68322-238-5

eBook Editions:
Adobe Digital Edition (.epub) 978-1-68322-539-3
Kindle and MobiPocket Edition (.prc) 978-1-68322-540-9

Published by Barbour Books, an imprint of Barbour Publishing, Inc., 1810 Barbour Drive, Uhrichsville, Ohio 44683, www.barbourbooks.com

Our mission is to inspire the world with the life-changing message of the Bible.

Member of the
Evangelical Christian
Publishers Association

Printed in the United States of America.
06076 0418 BP

*Your word is a lamp to guide
my feet and a light for my path.*

PSALM 119:105 NLT

Introduction

Wouldn't it be wonderful if you could hear the voice of the Lord whispering words *yes!* of encouragement in your ear? You can, through His Word, the Bible. He also speaks to your heart, though the words can't be heard with your ears.

This wonderful devotional will make you feel as if Jesus Himself were speaking the words to you, His daughter. Picture Him sitting nearby, sharing from His heart to yours as you read these devotions.

These devotions aren't supposed to take the place of your Bible-reading time. They're just a sweet way for the scriptures to come to life. They will also help you form the habit of spending time with God every day.

Here's a really cool idea: Why not share what you learn in this devotional with your school friends, family members, and even the girls you don't usually talk to? Everyone needs inspiration and encouragement, and everyone needs to understand that Jesus loves them. . .truly, truly loves them.

Knocking on Your Heart's Door

. . . .

I am standing just outside your door. It's
true! I know you can't see Me with your eyes,
but if you're listening—really listening—you
will hear My voice. You'll hear it through the *yes*
words in the Bible and in your heart. Are ✓
your ears open to the sound of My knock?
If so, then open wide the door of your
(heart) mind, and soul so that we can spend
wonderful time together. That's what I love
more than anything, sweet girl—spending
time with you. Why? Because I adore you! I
can never get enough Father-daughter time!

Of course, spending time together might
mean you'll have to make extra time in your
schedule. Some girls meet with Me in the
morning, before school. Others pray in the
evenings, just before bed. I'm happy to
be with you no matter what time of day. I
promise, the time we spend together will
be so enjoyable. Do you hear Me tap, tap,
tapping on your heart's door? If so, then
come! Come and climb in My lap for some
sweet conversations. I can't wait to hang
out with you. I hope you feel the same!

Behold, I stand at the door
and knock; if anyone hears and
listens to and heeds My voice
and opens the door, I will come
in to him and will eat with him,
and he [will eat] with Me.

REVELATION 3:20 AMPC

. . . .

Puffed Up

. . . .

Every girl wants to think highly of herself. That's human nature. I created you to love yourself, after all. But when you begin to spend too much time thinking about how great you are (or compare yourself to others), then you've become prideful. I don't want any of My girls to be puffed up, to think they're better than others. In fact, My Word, the Bible, is filled with scriptures about loving others as you love yourself.

So what does that mean? To love others as you love yourself does mean you have to care about yourself, too. But loving others requires sacrifice. It means you have to be willing to go the extra mile. Treat people kindly. Make sure you brag about their gifts and abilities as much as or more than your own. Make sure they feel special. . .because they are.

Does this mean you shouldn't be proud of your accomplishments? Of course not! I'm thrilled when you do great things, and you should feel confident, too. But remember to place your confidence in Me, not yourself. When you do that, then pride vanishes.

Nothing should be done because
of pride or thinking about yourself.
Think of other people as more
important than yourself.

PHILIPPIANS 2:3 NLV

The Road Is Narrow

. . . .

Imagine you're riding your new bike down a wide trail. All of a sudden the trail begins to narrow. It's not as wide as it once was. Then, as you keep riding, you notice it's getting narrower and narrower. Before long, there's barely enough space for the bike to get through.

That's kind of how it is when you live for Me. The road to heaven is narrow. There's really only one way to get there: you have to accept Me as your Lord and Savior and choose to live for Me. Others around you (your friends, neighbors, and so on) might be on a wide road. They might think there are several ways to get to heaven. But you know the truth, and you can share that news with them. Yes, the road is narrow, but it's a wonderful road, filled with twists and turns and lots of adventures along the way. We're going to have a blast following this road together. So what's keeping you? Go on! Tell others about the narrow road.

"Enter by the narrow gate.
For the gate is wide and the way is easy
that leads to destruction, and those who
enter by it are many. For the gate is
narrow and the way is hard that leads
to life, and those who find it are few.'

MATTHEW 7:13–14 ESV

· ·

Loving Others

. . . .

Some people think that loving others is easy, and oftentimes that is the case. But not everyone is easy to love. Sure, loving those who are sweet to you is a piece of cake, but what about loving those who aren't so nice to you?

I want all of My girls to treat others with love, even people who are really, really tough to get along with. Want to know how to do that? Just follow My example. Read My book, the Bible, and see all of the many, many stories about the times I stopped along My journey to care for others in need. You will find that I went out of My way to love people, even the most unlovable people!

You can do it. You can love those who are easy to love and the ones who are tough. I know because I have loved you, even on the days when you've been tough to love. So keep trying. Don't give up on the people who make it difficult. When you feel like you can't keep loving, just pray and I'll give you the strength and the courage to love them no matter what.

"A new commandment I give to you,
that you love one another:
just as I have loved you,
you also are to love one another."

JOHN 13:34 ESV

. . . .

In the World

. . . .

I placed you in this wonderful world that I created, surrounded by millions of people who are all very different. And I've asked you in My Word to be *in* the world but not *of* the world. What does that mean, exactly? Why would I have placed you here (and not on the moon or on Jupiter or someplace like that)?

To be "in" the world means that you live on planet Earth. Your house is here, your school is here, and the people you love are here. Aren't you glad about that? Wouldn't it be awkward if fun Aunt Susie lived on Saturn and not Earth?

Yes, you live in the world I've created for you. But I don't want you to be "of" the world. I don't want you to be like others. When you follow after others, you dress like they dress, talk like they talk, act like they act. It's tempting to want to be of the world, but that's not how My girls should live. You should be different from everyone. I want you to set an example. Speak differently. Act differently. When people around you are mean-spirited, respond with kindness. When your friends use bad language, don't go along with them. There are enough copycats in the world, trust Me. I've made you to be different. So do your best to live by My example. You'll do a fine job, sweet girl!

"If you were of the world, the world would love you as its own; but because you are not of the world, but I chose you out of the world, therefore the world hates you.'

JOHN 15:19 ESV

Forgiveness

. . . .

Oh, sweet girl! I know it's so hard to forgive people when they hurt your feelings. I've been there, so I understand. People can be so mean, and they say such hurtful things. But I want you to take a deep breath and remember all of the many, many times I've forgiven you when you've hurt others. Aren't you grateful I chose to let go of the pain you caused?

Why is it always best to forgive? Because when you choose *not* to forgive, you're really hurting yourself, not others. It's true. You get angry on the inside, and before long it affects everything you do. It even affects your health! I don't want you to suffer any more than you already have, so I've come up with a better way and I've called it "forgiveness."

When you forgive, you let go of the bitterness. You give it to Me. You trust Me to take care of the situation. And you are free to live your life without fretting over what that person has done to you. It's not your problem anymore. It's Mine.

So do your best to let go. Ask for My help. I'll give it to you, I promise.

Be kind to one another,
tenderhearted, forgiving one another,
as God in Christ forgave you.

EPHESIANS 4:32 ESV

A Cheerful Giver

. . . .

I love a cheerful giver! It makes Me want to smile every time I see you doing something kind and generous for others. When you're wrapping a gift for a friend. When you're feeding the homeless. When you're taking a special gift to an elderly person. When you're sending a thank-you note to your mom. I love all of that. I also love it when you decide to give offerings at church or donate to missionaries.

Here's the thing about giving: it has to be your idea, not something you're forced to do. Need an example? Imagine you earned $40 working for your dad. You wanted to buy a great new gadget with it, but your dad suggested you give part of it to the church first. You know that giving part of it away is a good idea (and I agree), but you don't really want to do it. You say yes with your mouth, but in your heart you're really upset. You finally give an offering to the church, but you grumble the whole time.

How much better would it be if you made up your mind to give. . .and give cheerfully! Then we'd both be happy. And here's a fun nugget of truth that you'll find in

My Word, the Bible: When you give, I give back to you. In other words, if you cheerfully give to Me, I bless you in return.

So go on. . .give with a cheerful heart. Then watch as I shower down blessings on you in response!

Each one must give as he has decided in his heart, not reluctantly or under compulsion, for God loves a cheerful giver.

2 CORINTHIANS 9:7 ESV

Making Good Choices

· · · · · · · · · · · · · · · · · · ·

Choices, choices! They're everywhere, aren't they? Every time you're sitting in class and you're tempted to sneak a peek at your friend's paper, you have a choice to make! Whenever you're tempted to argue with your mom or fight with your little brother, you face more choices. Choices are a part of life, and I'm so thrilled when you make the right ones. You can choose not to cheat. You can choose not to argue. You can choose not to fight.

How do I know this? Because I created you in My image, and I'm not a fighter! I made you to be like Me—loving, gracious, and kind. I've also given you My Spirit, to give you courage and power to make better choices.

Need an example of some great choices you can make? Choose to be obedient to your parents and other authorities. Choose to do your best work in school. Choose the right kind of friends. Choose to set an example for others in how you live. Choose to spend time with Me daily. Choose to praise Me, even when things aren't going your way. Now those are some great choices!

The right choice is always the right choice, even when it's hard. But don't worry. I'll help you. Don't give in to the temptation to do the wrong thing. Just remember, I made you to make good choices.

Many are the plans in the mind of a man, but it is the purpose of the LORD that will stand.

PROVERBS 19:21 ESV

. . . .

Talking to God

. . . .

You love to talk! I know this because I hear every word. When you talk to your mom, I hear you! When you giggle with your friends, I hear that, too! And when you talk to your brothers and sisters, I hear that (even when you argue). I love to listen to you talk.

Guess who I really, really love hearing you talk to? Me! That's right, Me! I'm especially thrilled when you come to Me first with your problems before sharing with anyone else. It makes Me feel so good to know that you trust Me with all the things you're going through.

I care, you know. It's hard to imagine, but I care even more than your parents, your grandparents, your teachers, or your friends. The kind of love that I have for you goes above and beyond what you can imagine. So trust Me when I say that talking to Me is the safest thing you can do. And when you tell Me the things that are troubling you, I take action. I don't just listen and then walk away. You can count on Me to do something. So open up! Start talking, girl. I love to hear your sweet voice.

"If my people who are called by my name humble themselves, and pray and seek my face and turn from their wicked ways, then I will hear from heaven and will forgive their sin and heal their land.'

2 CHRONICLES 7:14 ESV

. . . .

Created to Worship Me

· · · · · · · · · · · · · · · · ·

Do you know what it means to worship? When you worship something, you give it your full attention. You're not distracted by the things around you. Some people worship weird things. . .like money. Oh, they don't bow down and pray to it, but they worship it by caring too much about it. And others worship their friends. They care more about their friendships than they do about Me. Some people worship their possessions. They love their stuff so much that it means the world to them.

None of these things should be worshipped. In fact, nothing should mean more to you than Me. I need to be first in your life. I created you to worship Me. It's true! I love you so much, and it makes My heart happy when you love Me back.

So how do you worship Me? With your words, of course. You can start by saying things like, "I love You, Lord!" and "Lord, I praise You!" (What a great way to start your conversation with Me!) I also love it when you worship by singing songs of praise. Your voice sounds like an angel choir to Me! And boy, do I get tickled when you praise Me by telling others about Me. That makes My heart so happy. Of course, I'm also thrilled when you choose to praise Me by loving others. That's a great way to worship. So go ahead! Worship Me with your whole heart!

My mouth is filled with your praise,
and with your glory all the day.
PSALM 71:8 ESV

Love Never Fails

. . . .

Have you ever made a failing grade in school? Picture this: You stay up late working on your homework. Then you wake up the next morning and rush to get ready for school. Because you're in a hurry, you accidentally leave your backpack at home. Your homework is in the backpack. You hope your mom will realize and bring the backpack to school, but she's at work and doesn't know. You try to explain to your teacher, but she won't let you bring it tomorrow. Instead, she gives you a big fat F. You're humiliated! How could she give you a failing grade when you did the hard work? It doesn't seem fair!

In some ways, that's what life is like. You try so hard to do so many things. You work, work, work, but still come out with a big fat F many times. Not everything works out the way you hope. But there's one thing that never, ever fails: love. Showing love to others will get you an A every time!

So make up your mind to shower love on people, even when they don't deserve it. It makes My heart happy when you go out of your way to love the unlovable. That's what I've done, after all. Love. . .it never fails!

And to all these things, you must
add love. Love holds everything
and everybody together and makes
all these good things perfect.

COLOSSIANS 3:14 NLV

. . . .

Planting Seeds

. . . .

It's so much fun to plant seeds in the ground and watch them grow. I know you enjoy watching things spring to life. If you think about what the farmer does, you'll know what I mean. He takes that tiny little seed, so dry and small, and places it in the soil. Then he presses it down and covers it with dirt. Afterward, he waters the soil and then waters it again. Then the sun shines down on the patch of dirt. Day after day he waters the seed. Day after day, the sun does its part. Finally, at just the right time, a little bit of green pops up! Soon the farmer sees a gorgeous flower, colorful and bright.

What does this have to do with you? I want you to be a seed planter. How do you do that? Start by sharing the news of what I've done in your life. When you tell others about Me, you're planting seeds! Then water those seeds with love. Then wait for the sun (Me!) to shine down on the seeds until they spring to life. At just the right time, you'll see your friends and loved ones blossom like beautiful flowers. . .and all because you took the time to plant some seeds.

For as the soil makes the sprout
come up and a garden causes seeds to
grow, so the Sovereign LORD will
make righteousness and praise
spring up before all nations.

ISAIAH 61:11 NIV

A Lot to Offer

. . . .

I see you! I see all the way down into your heart. And I know what you're thinking and feeling. You're thinking, *I don't have much to offer. What gifts and talents do I have?* Oh, but you do! You have a lot to offer people. If anyone knows this, I do! I created you, after all, and gave you many, many special talents and abilities. Some of them don't even require practice.

Why not offer people a bright smile, a cheerful "Hello!" or a little wave? Why not go out of your way to share your lunch with a friend who forgot hers or help your little brother learn his multiplication tables? Or maybe you could spend a Saturday morning helping your mom mop the kitchen floor or work in the backyard with Dad, pulling weeds in the garden.

Of course, you have other great things to offer, too. I also give My girls special artistic gifts that they can use for Me—acting, singing, dancing, and so on. You can use these gifts to share My love and to spread the good news about My love.

Yes, sweet girl, you have a lot to offer. So stop looking at the things you *can't* do and start looking at the things you *can*.

As each has received a gift,
use it to serve one another, as good
stewards of God's varied grace.

1 PETER 4:10 ESV

. . . .

Faithful over a Little

If you're faithful over the little things, I will end up giving you more and more. It's true! Are you wondering what I mean by that?

Imagine your mom gave you a dollar. You decided not to spend it. Instead, you put it in the bank and kept adding a little bit more money to it. Before long, you had ten dollars. Then twenty. Then, before you knew it, a hundred dollars or more! That's how it works. Because you were faithful and diligent with that teensy-tiny dollar, it grew and grew and grew!

It's the same way with responsibility. If you handle responsibility well, if you're faithful and diligent, I'll make sure you end up with more opportunities over time. I love it when My girls prove that they can be faithful with the little things. Why? Because I know bigger things are coming. So hang on, girl! Be faithful with the tasks you're facing right now. I can promise you, much bigger things are headed your way if you'll remain faithful.

"His master said to him,
'Well done, good and faithful
servant. You have been faithful over
a little; I will set you over much.
Enter into the joy of your master.'"

MATTHEW 25:21 ESV

Mean Girls

. . . .

I wish all of My children would be kind to one another, but not everyone feels the same way. In fact, some people are just plain mean. I see how they treat others, and it breaks My heart. In fact, I've seen how some girls have treated you at times, and it makes Me so sad. I don't want your heart to hurt over the things that mean girls say and do, but I see that you're often wounded by ugly words and actions.

Here's My solution to mean girls: love them. I know it's going to be hard, but you can do it with My help. Love them when they say mean things. Treat them with kindness, even when they treat you badly. Turn the other cheek. That's My plan for success in your life.

I know it makes no sense, but trust Me. I promise you'll be happy with the way things turn out. If you treat others the way you want to be treated, those girls with mean hearts can be changed from the inside out. Before long, those meanies will be sweeter than sugar, if you lead by example.

Beloved, if God so loved us,
we also ought to love one another.

1 JOHN 4:11 ESV

· ·

Creation

. . . .

What do you think of My creation, sweet girl? Look around you. The gorgeous leaves on the trees. The colorful flowers. The smile on a baby's face. Your reflection in the mirror. These are all signs of My precious creation.

Did you know that I created all of nature to praise Me? It's true. The rocks. The trees. The bushes. The birds in the sky. They are all giving praise to Me, whether you hear it or not. The sound of the crickets chirping? It's praise! The rippling water in the brook? It's praising Me, too!

I'm a very creative God. I loved coming up with all of the animals, the fish, the birds, and the trees. I had a blast thinking up the colors of the rainbow and the way the sun would feel as it shines on your face. What fun to create all of that with you in mind. I'm so glad you love and care for My creation. Thank you for that! I'm very pleased that you are enjoying the things I worked so hard to create just for you. And remember, I created you, too! You're a part of My wonderful creation!

"Worthy are you, our Lord and God,
to receive glory and honor and power,
for you created all things, and by your
will they existed and were created.'

REVELATION 4:11 ESV

....

All Things New

. . . .

Do you ever wish you could have a do-over? I'm sure you do! I've seen you lose your temper and yell at people. I've seen you treat others poorly and then regret it. I've seen you fall down on the job and then wish you'd given it your all. Time and time again you've made mistakes and then wished you could start over again and make things right.

All of My children wish they could do things over again at times, no matter how old they are. Even grown-ups struggle with this. You would be shocked if I told you how many adults ask Me for a do-over! So it's not just kids, trust Me!

Here's some good news for you: I give lots of second chances. And third chances. And fourth! In fact, I keep giving more chances because I love you and want you to grow in your faith.

Don't give up. Just try again. I'll be right there with you, whispering, "You can do this!" in your ear. So give it another try. Then another. I'll make all things new, no matter how rough things have been. That's a promise from Me to you because I love you.

"For I know the plans I have for you,'
declares the LORD, "plans to prosper
you and not to harm you, plans to
give you hope and a future.'

JEREMIAH 29:11 NIV

. . . .

Jigsaw Puzzle

. . . .

I know, I know! You sometimes look at your life and feel like there are missing puzzle pieces. The picture isn't clear. Oh, you can see parts of it, but not all. Bits of it are fuzzy. Not everything seems to come together the way you think it should. But don't worry, sweet girl! I can see the picture very clearly, and I'm already working hard to fit the pieces together so that they make sense, not just to you, but to everyone around you.

Want to know a secret? I care very much about how things turn out for you. I do. It makes Me smile just thinking about how surprised you'll be when you see how I'm working things together for your good. So don't fret! Just trust Me, even when it's really, really hard. Pretty soon you'll see the whole picture. It won't be a puzzle any longer. And what you see will surprise and delight you, I promise!

Why would I work so hard to make things perfect for you? Because I love you, that's why!

And we know that in all things
God works for the good of those
who love him, who have been
called according to his purpose.

ROMANS 8:28 NIV

. . . .

God's Will

. . . .

Do you know what it means to be stubborn? A stubborn girl wants things her own way. She wants what she wants, and she wants it now. Have you ever been like that? Don't deny it! I can see inside your heart, after all. I've seen you stamp your foot and demand your own way. I've seen you argue with people and try to convince them that you're right, even when you know in your heart that you're not.

Everyone wants their own way at times. It's just human nature. But it's important to remember that My way is best. That's why I want you to change the way you're praying. No more stubbornness or selfishness when you talk to Me! From now on, instead of just telling Me what to do (or what you want), try adding the words, "Your will be done."

When you pray for My will, not your own, things will work out much better for you. How do you know? Because I adore you! I want even better things for you than you could ever think of on your own. So from now on it's My way. . .all the way. Lay down your stubbornness. Don't insist on having your own way. Can you deal with that, sweet girl? Good! Because great things are heading your way if you dare to believe that My way is best.

Give thanks in all circumstances; for this is God's will for you in Christ Jesus.

1 THESSALONIANS 5:18 NIV

· ·

Confidence

. . . .

Look around you! All around you will see people with their heads up high, walking with confidence. At least they appear to be. And I see your heart: I know you're wondering if you will ever feel that courageous. Your friends tell you to be confident in yourself, in your own abilities, but it doesn't seem to work. You're not feeling any more confident, though you try and try.

The only way you can be truly confident is to put your trust in Me. This means you don't depend on yourself when things are hard. You don't go around trying to fix every situation. You admit that you don't have all the answers. I'm the biggest of the big, and I can fix anything. And I don't even have to fake it!

So where do you start? Pray. Give Me your problems and concerns, then watch as I give you all the confidence you need to face anything life throws your way. I love you. I'm just reminding you of that fact! Through Me, you can do anything, so hold that head high!

Though an army besiege me,
my heart will not fear;
though war break out against me,
even then I will be confident.

PSALM 27:3 NIV

. . . .

Addiction

. . . .

To be addicted to something means you can't seem to give it up, no matter how hard you try. Some people would say that "addiction" is a grown-up word and that only adults deal with this problem. But that's not true. A lot of My kiddos are addicted to things like electronics, sugar, television shows, and so on. They try and try to quit, but can't do it on their own.

Don't believe Me? What if I said, "You have to give up your favorite candy," or "You have to give up those video games"? What would you do? Or what if I said, "It's time to give up eating ice cream," or "No more chewing gum!"? You might panic, right? The truth is, I don't like to see you addicted to anything. . .but Me!

Sometimes it's fun to challenge yourself, to see if you can give up something you love. It's a good way to tell if you're addicted. For example, you might give up video games for a few days just to see if you can. Don't worry. I'll help you. If you trust Me, addictions can be a thing of the past.

No temptation has overtaken you that is not common to man. God is faithful, and he will not let you be tempted beyond your ability, but with the temptation he will also provide the way of escape, that you may be able to endure it.

1 CORINTHIANS 10:13 ESV

· ·

Self-Control

. . . .

I saw that! You told yourself you wouldn't eat that donut, but you did it anyway! And that time you promised yourself you wouldn't be mean to your friend but you just couldn't seem to help yourself? I saw that, too. Am I disappointed in you? Oh, maybe a little, but I have an easy answer for your problem: stop trying to do things on your own.

I know, I know! Everyone around you says, "Use your self-control!" or "You can do this on your own. Just try harder." But the truth is, without Me you can't accomplish very much. If you ask for My help, I will give it, I promise. You won't have to depend on self-control; you can have God-control. And I promise you, My control is a lot better because I love you even more than you love yourself and I want you to succeed.

So what are you waiting for, sweet girl? Give the control to Me and let Me take it from here. Hand Me the reins of your life and let Me drive the cart! I promise you won't be disappointed with the results.

"For my thoughts are not your thoughts, neither are your ways my ways, declares the LORD. For as the heavens are higher than the earth, so are my ways higher than your ways and my thoughts than your thoughts."

ISAIAH 55:8–9 ESV

. . . .

Bringing Down the Walls

. . . .

Did you realize that you have walls up around you? It's true! And I'm not just talking about the kind in your house. Sometimes you put up emotional walls—to keep people out. They grow taller, taller, taller with each passing day.

Want an example? Remember that time you got your feelings hurt and you made up your mind never to let someone do that to you again? Remember how you pulled away from the person who had hurt you? You put up walls so that no one could ever injure you again. I saw all of that, and I see the walls that are still up around your heart. You think you're protecting yourself, but that simply isn't the case. If you'll trust Me, I'll do the protecting, I promise!

I would love to bring those walls down, sweet girl. Don't worry! Remember what I just said? I'll take care of you. With just one word from you, I'll demolish those walls and sweep in with My Holy Spirit to guard and protect your heart. So what's holding you back? Go ahead. . .ask! I'm standing nearby, just waiting to tear those walls down.

We do live in the world, but we do not fight in the same way the world fights. We fight with weapons that are different from those the world uses. Our weapons have power from God that can destroy the enemy's strong places. We destroy people's arguments and every proud thing that raises itself against the knowledge of God. We capture every thought and make it give up and obey Christ.

2 CORINTHIANS 10:3–5 NCV

Make Lemonade

. . . .

Things don't always work out the way you plan, do they? I've been watching, and I see how disappointed you are when things go wrong. But here's a fun secret: when life gives you lemons—sour things or bad things—you can make lemonade out of them! In other words, you can turn the sour things into something sweet.

Want an example? Remember that time you were hoping your family could go to Disney World and it didn't work out? Instead, you were stuck at home for a week? Sour experience, right? Well, here's how you could have turned it into something sweet: You could have spent that whole week planning fun activities for your family to do. Maybe you could have turned your backyard into an amusement park or created some fun costumes for your brothers and sisters to wear. Maybe you could have donated your time at a homeless shelter, working alongside Mom and Dad to feed people who don't have food.

It's all how you look at it, sweet girl! Even the sour situations can be sweetened if you use your imagination! So don't let the bitter times get you down. Just watch and see how I can sweeten them, if you put your trust in Me.

Always be joyful. Pray continually, and give thanks whatever happens. That is what God wants for you in Christ Jesus.

1 THESSALONIANS 5:16–18 NCV

. . . .

Modesty

. . . .

What comes to mind when you hear the word *modesty*? Some people think it has to do with your wardrobe. Others think it has to do with the way you live. Want to know a little secret? It's both!

My girls do need to be careful with what they wear. Why? Because they represent Me! This means you have to double-check what you're wearing in the mirror before you leave the house. Don't wear your clothes too tight or your skirts too short. Choose your wardrobe wisely. Don't do anything to draw negative attention to yourself. Wear clothes that show your sweet personality.

Use modesty in the rest of your life, too. Use modest speech. No rough jokes. No swearing. No making fun of others. No pushing others around. Just loving, sweet words that reflect My heart for others. If you live in a way that shows My life, you'll make My heart very, very happy. A modest girl makes for a very happy family!

Likewise also that women should adorn
themselves in respectable apparel,
with modesty and self-control,
not with braided hair and gold
or pearls or costly attire.

1 TIMOTHY 2:9 ESV

. . . .

Making Time for Me

. . . .

Have you ever wondered why I decided to create daytime and nighttime? And why are there twenty-four hours in a day? Why not ten or twelve? I decided that the twenty-four-hour plan would give you—My children—plenty of time to work, rest, and play. More important, it gives you lots of time to spend with Me.

So how do I want you to spend our time together? It would be really fun if you would start by singing a song of praise to Me. I love it when My girls sing! And then you could open your Bible, My Word, and read some verses. You might be very, very surprised because I can make certain verses jump out at you. For example, if you're struggling to forgive a friend for something she did, I can point out a verse about the importance of forgiveness. (I love to surprise you with verses like that!) Finally, we can spend some time talking to each other. You share your heart with Me (telling Me your troubles, asking for My help, thanking Me for the gifts I've given you), and then I will talk back (whispering things like "I love you!" to your heart).

I've given you plenty of time to spend with Me, and I miss you when you don't show up for our get-togethers, so let's make a plan to meet. . .soon!

But when you pray, go into your room and shut the door and pray to your Father who is in secret. And your Father who sees in secret will reward you.

MATTHEW 6:6 ESV

My Word

Did you know that the Bible is one of the many ways I talk to you? It's true! When you don't know what to do, just open the Bible and look for a verse that will guide you!

Need an example? Let's say you're struggling with a friend who's hurt your feelings. You can't seem to forgive her. Your parents talk to you about it, but you still can't seem to let it go. After all, your friend really, really hurt your feelings. What do you do? You pray, of course, and then you open your Bible and stumble upon this scripture: "But if you don't forgive other people, then your Father in heaven will not forgive your sins" (Mark 11:26 NCV).

Oops! "You mean I have to forgive others or God won't forgive me?" you ask. The answer is yes. That's My best plan for you. Forgive. . .and I will forgive you. And just think, you never would have known that if you hadn't opened your Bible! My Word is filled with priceless treasures like this. So dig in! You have a lot to learn.

God's word is alive and working and is
sharper than a double-edged sword.
It cuts all the way into us, where the soul
and the spirit are joined, to the center of
our joints and bones. And it judges the
thoughts and feelings in our hearts.

HEBREWS 4:12 NCV

. . . .

Be Yourself

. . . .

It's fun to play-act sometimes, isn't it? If you've ever been to a costume party (or gone trick-or-treating as a character from a movie), then you know how fun it is to pretend to be someone you're not. Maybe you dressed up like a superhero or a fairy. Perhaps you wore an angel costume or decided to go as Cinderella. No matter who you pretended to be, you had the time of your life!

Yes, it's fun to pretend to be someone else, especially someone with superpowers, but here's a little secret: it's better to be yourself. It's true! I like it when My girls are content to be themselves. It breaks My heart to see you try, try, try to be like others, especially the girls you know from school or your neighborhood. I love you just like you are! You don't need to change anything about yourself in order to get Me to love you more. I love you to the moon already! So no pretending. . .unless you're dressing up in a costume. Just be yourself. It's who I created you to be!

Do not be conformed to this world,
but be transformed by the renewal of
your mind, that by testing you may
discern what is the will of God,
what is good and acceptable and perfect.

ROMANS 12:2 ESV

. . . .

Try, Try Again

. . . .

I see how hard it is to keep trying, sweet girl. You try so many different things—sports, singing, acting—and then you think it's too hard. The same happens in school. You struggle in math class or reading, and you feel like giving up.

Here's the thing about giving up. If you quit too soon, before you've really tried your hardest, you might miss out on something really special! Think about all the great Olympic athletes. What if Gabby Douglas had given up on gymnastics? What if Michael Phelps had quit swimming? What if Tara Lipinski had stopped ice-skating? All of these people faced tough days but kept going anyway. In other words, they didn't give up. And you shouldn't, either! Even when things get hard, keep trying.

If you get discouraged, just say the words "Try, try again." Then put some action behind those words. Get going, girl! You can do it!

And let us not grow weary
of doing good, for in due season
we will reap, if we do not give up.

GALATIANS 6:9 ESV

....

Erasing Your Past

. . . .

I know you better than anyone else does, even the people you live with. (Hard to believe, I know!) They can see what's on the outside—your hair color, your clothes, and so on, but I see much deeper, straight to your heart. I know when you're hurting, when you're pretending to be okay, even though you're not. I know about all the times when you messed up and wished you could have a do-over.

That time you hurt your sister's feelings and wished you could make it up to her? I saw that. And the time you argued with your mom and then felt bad afterward? I was right there, listening in! You have a precious heart, and you want to get things right, even on the days when you make mistakes.

I have great news for you, sweet girl! You can have a do-over! When I went to the cross in your place, I carried all of your mess-ups with Me. I really did! I took the penalty so that you could live in forgiveness. All you have to do is ask.

Brethren, I do not regard myself as
having laid hold of it yet; but one thing
I do: forgetting what lies behind and
reaching forward to what lies ahead,
I press on toward the goal for the prize of
the upward call of God in Christ Jesus.

PHILIPPIANS 3:13–14 NASB

Appreciation

. . . .

Everyone wants to be appreciated. What if
you took the time to do something really
nice for a friend or loved one. . .maybe you
saved your money and bought a very special
gift. Then imagine that friend took the gift,
smiled, and said nothing. No "Thank you."
No "Wow, this is great!" Nothing. Or worse!
Imagine she looked at your gift, shrugged,
and said, "I don't really like this," and then
gave it back to you. You would be upset,
right? And rightfully so!

When people take the time to say thank
you (and really mean it), you feel good about
what you've done.

Now let's think about that in reverse.
Sometimes I see your parents doing a lot for
you. They work hard all day, prepare your
meals, wash your clothes, help you with
homework, drive you to athletic practices
or ballet class. How do you respond?
Sometimes you're grateful, but many
days you forget to say thank you. So pay
attention. Tomorrow when your parents work
hard for you, take the time to show them
some appreciation. Doing so will make Me
(and them) very, very happy.

Let the word of Christ dwell in you
richly, teaching and admonishing one
another in all wisdom, singing psalms
and hymns and spiritual songs,
with thankfulness in your hearts to God.

COLOSSIANS 3:16 ESV

. . . .

A Quick Study

. . . .

You're a quick study. That means it doesn't take you long to catch on. When you learn fast, I don't have to repeat Myself, and that's a good thing. Of course, not everyone is a quick study! Some people don't ever seem to learn their lessons.

Want an example? What if you decided to cheat on a test in school? Not good, right? Now imagine that I whispered in your ear, "Please don't do that again. It makes Me very sad, and it sets a bad example for others." Only you pretended not to hear My voice. You just ignored Me and decided to cheat once again during the next test. Maybe you leaned over and copied from the girl sitting next to you and you got away with it once again, so you kept cheating, even though I kept whispering in your ear, "Don't do it! What you're doing is wrong!"

Someone who knows what they're doing is wrong but keeps doing it anyway is living in sin, and that breaks My heart. That person is not a quick study. In fact, some of those people never seem to learn their lesson.

You can be different! Keep being a fast learner, girl! It makes Me smile when I don't have to repeat Myself!

Be diligent to present yourself
approved to God as a workman
who does not need to be ashamed,
accurately handling the word of truth.

2 TIMOTHY 2:15 NASB

. . . .

Pretty from the Inside Out

. . . .

I see how you are. You want to be pretty. Well, here's some fun news. . .you are! No matter what you look like on the outside, you're beautiful to Me. It's true. You're more gorgeous than any supermodel. Want to know why? You're created in My image, and all of My kids are gorgeous!

I know that girls your age think they have to look a certain way or dress a certain way, but here's the truth: I'm far more concerned about how pretty you are on the inside than how you look on the outside. A gorgeous heart is more impressive than a great new outfit or a beautiful hairdo. It's definitely lovelier than anything hanging in your closet.

So go ahead and wear your favorite outfit. Fix your hair. Put on your brightest smile. But remember, it's truly what's on the inside that counts the most. Keep that in mind and you'll be the prettiest girl on the block!

[Christ] gave up his life for [the church]
to make her holy and clean, washed
by the cleansing of God's word.
He did this to present her to himself as
a glorious church without a spot or
wrinkle or any other blemish.
Instead, she will be holy and without fault.

EPHESIANS 5:25–27 NLT

· ·

Trust

· · · · · · · · · · · · · · · · · ·

Do you trust Me, sweet girl? It's an important question, I know. I want all of My girls to know they can trust Me no matter what they're going through. Sometimes people forget. They see the bad stuff that's going on around them and think I've disappeared like a puff of smoke. It's not true, though. I'm right here beside you, even when you're going through hard things.

Do you know what it means to really, really trust? To have faith? It means that you believe in something you cannot see. So even if you don't see Me with your eyes—and you don't—you can trust that I'm with you because I've promised in My Word, the Bible, that I will never leave you or forsake you. You can count on that. Don't count on your eyes to tell you what's true and what isn't. Count on your heart and your spirit. And remember, if I said it, you can believe it!

But when you ask him, be sure that your
faith is in God alone. Do not waver,
for a person with divided loyalty is as
unsettled as a wave of the sea that is
blown and tossed by the wind.

JAMES 1:6 NLT

Sleepyhead

. . . .

I see you yawning, sleepyhead! And I don't blame you. Life can be really tiring! You're such a busy girl—school, activities, family events, spending time with friends, church, sports, homework. Whew! No wonder you're exhausted sometimes. It's enough to make a person tired just reading your schedule.

Did you ever wonder why I created your body to need sleep? I didn't have to do it that way, you know. I could've created a body that didn't need any rest at all, but I chose to design you in My image, and even I take breaks. Don't believe it? Read the book of Genesis (the first book in the Bible). You'll see that I worked for six days to create the world. Talk about a lot of work! Then I rested on the seventh day. In other words, I took a much-needed break!

You need a break, too, so learn from My example. You need to get plenty of sleep at night and even have times of rest during the day. So don't fight it! Stop yawning and climb in bed for a nap. You're going to need it! I've got big things planned for you, after all!

Return to your rest,
O my soul, for the LORD
has dealt bountifully with you.

PSALM 116:7 NKJV

. . . .

Making Fun of Others

. . . .

Picture this: You're hanging out with your friends having lunch at school when you see a girl sitting alone at a nearby table. No one wants to hang out with her. She doesn't really dress like the other kids in school, and maybe she talks or acts different. Someone in your group starts to make fun of her. At first you're a little scared to say anything. You don't want to stir up anything with your friends, so you just listen in as they poke fun at her.

After a while they talk you into doing it, too. Then just about the time the lunch period ends, you all go up to the girl and say mean things to her about what she's wearing. You know in your heart you shouldn't, but going along with the crowd just seems easier. You can see the tears in the girl's eyes. You can tell she's going to cry as soon as you all walk away, and you feel terrible. . .but stopping seems so hard.

I need you to know something. When I see this kind of behavior from My girls—especially girls like you who tell others that they're My kids—it completely breaks My heart. Totally and completely. Instead of cutting others down, I would love to see you build them up. Instead of poking fun at that girl, you should have the opposite attitude from your friends. Making fun of others is completely off-limits. So be bold! Just say no to hateful words.

Just as damaging as a madman shooting a deadly weapon is someone who lies to a friend and then says, "I was only joking."

PROVERBS 26:18–19 NLT

Stuff

. . . .

Stuff, stuff. . .everywhere! I see it in your room. I see it under your bed. I see it in your closet. Sometimes I even see your stuff in other places around the house where it doesn't belong!

You've got a lot of stuff, girl! And you want even more. You see commercials on TV for the latest, greatest tablet or toy and you say to yourself, "Ooh, I'd love to have that!" Yep. You want more and more stuff.

Did you know there are girls in this world who have almost no stuff? It's true. There are really kids who have no money to buy toys or electronics or anything else. They don't go to the movies or eat snacks or take dance lessons. Many of those girls wouldn't know what to do with all that stuff, even if they did have it! They might look at it and say, "Why do I need all of that stuff anyway?"

The next time you think you want more, more, more. . .think about those girls who don't have much. It's not the stuff that matters, you know. Learning to be content with what you already have is a wonderful thing!

"Do not lay up for yourselves treasures on earth, where moth and rust destroy and where thieves break in and steal, but lay up for yourselves treasures in heaven, where neither moth nor rust destroys and where thieves do not break in and steal. For where your treasure is, there your heart will be also.'

MATTHEW 6:19–21 ESV

. . . .

Back to Basics

. . . .

Have you ever heard the phrase "back to basics"? To go back to basics means you go back to the very beginning and learn something all over again. Think of it like this: A baby learns to walk and then to run. If that baby broke his leg, he would have to go back to basics. . .learn to walk all over again. Make sense?

Sometimes you need to go back to basics, sweet girl. You need to relearn lessons you were taught before—lessons like "Love your neighbor as yourself" or "Obey your parents." Oh, I know. . .you already know all of that, but do you do it? If not, it might be time to start over again!

Starting over is nothing to be embarrassed about. It's certainly not a bad thing. In fact, I like for My kids to take a refresher course (to learn it all again). Keep working at it until it sticks! One of these days you won't have to relearn those lessons. You'll do the right thing because you've already learned it's the right thing to do!

Let the wise hear and increase in learning, and the one who understands obtain guidance.

PROVERBS 1:5 ESV

....

This Is a Test

. . . .

Taking tests in school isn't much fun, is it? You have to study, study, study. . .memorize, memorize, memorize! Whew! Talk about a challenge. And no matter how much you prepare, sometimes there are questions you just don't know the answer to. It hardly seems fair. After all, you worked so hard to get ready.

Sometimes life is like that, too. You go through seasons when it feels like your life is one big test, and you wonder if you're going to get any of the answers right. What sort of testing do I mean? Think about a time when someone you loved lost their job. And what about that time when someone in your family got sick, really, really sick? And remember that time when your friend moved away and you wondered if you'd ever make a new friend?

All of these times were "learning" times. I was watching to see how you would react, and you passed the test! That makes Me very happy, of course. But get ready, girl! There are more tests ahead.

"You study the Scriptures diligently
because you think that in them you
have eternal life. These are the very
Scriptures that testify about me.'

JOHN 5:39 NIV

. . . .

Selfie

· · · · · · · · · · · · · · · · ·

Taking selfies on your phone can be a lot of fun, right? I see all of those girls snapping pictures. Silly girls. They love to look at their own faces, I suppose. They're all about themselves.

Here's the thing about selfies. . .they're all in good fun, but when you get too focused on yourself and not on others, it's not such a good thing. Sometimes I wish My girls would spend more time focusing on the people around them and not themselves. That would make My heart happy.

How can you do that? Start by turning the camera around. See other people through the lens. Can you see the sad look on the woman's face as she walks by? Do you notice the elderly man in the wheelchair? Do you see the little boy who has no shoes? Can you make out the image of the girl with no friends?

If only you could see people the way I do, then you would give up on selfies and start loving people the way I love them. It's not too late. Turn that camera around, girl!

Beloved, let us love one another,
for love is of God; and everyone who
loves is born of God and knows God.

1 JOHN 4:7 NKJV

. . . .

Take Care of Yourself

· · · · · · · · · · · · · · · · · ·

There are so many things for My girls to take care of! Here are just a few: Schoolwork. Homework. Relationships. Keeping your room clean. Helping Mom and Dad around the house. Watching your little brother so that Mom can do the laundry. Whew! You stay really busy.

Here's a little secret: sometimes you're so busy taking care of everything (and everyone) else that you don't take very good care of yourself. Do you want to know what I mean by that? Sometimes you're moving so fast that you don't take the time to eat the right foods. Good, healthy foods are better for your body than pizza and ice cream and potato chips. And I see how crazy things get at bedtime. You want to get plenty of rest, but you have to finish your homework and get your clothes ready for tomorrow.

It's good to take care of things, but it's just as important to take care of you. Why? Because you're the only you you've got! There's not another copy of you in the closet, ready to come out! So watch what you eat, get plenty of rest, and you'll be in much better shape to take care of others.

Therefore I urge you, brethren,
by the mercies of God, to present your
bodies a living and holy sacrifice,
acceptable to God, which is your
spiritual service of worship.

ROMANS 12:1 NASB

. . . .

What Not to Wear

· · · · · · · · · · · · · · · · · ·

Girls sure love fashion, don't they? They're always looking at shirts and jeans and shoes and all sorts of jewelry. They love shopping in stores and looking at pictures of clothes in magazines, too. There's nothing wrong with that, but let Me clue you in on a secret: I'm far more interested in a different kind of fashion, the kind you can't see with your eyes.

Are you wondering what I mean by that? I'm talking about dressing yourself in love. Yes, you can put on love the same way you put on a necklace! And joy. Do you dress yourself in joy every day? And what about peace? Do you dress yourself in peace? All of these things I'm talking about are very, very important to Me. I'm not as concerned about the way you wear your hair. I'm much more concerned about how you wear your heart.

Maybe it's time for a fashion show, girl! Show those friends of yours what it's like to dress in the things that matter to Me. Maybe they'll learn that being trendy isn't all it's cracked up to be. A true fashion statement is one that makes My heart happy.

Above all, clothe yourselves
with love, which binds us all
together in perfect harmony.

COLOSSIANS 3:14 NLT

. . . .

A Tight Squeeze

. . . .

Have you ever tried to put on a shirt that doesn't fit anymore? You s-q-u-e-e-z-e, but it just doesn't work. In fact, it's downright painful! Before long you hear a terrible ripping sound. You look down and discover that the seams on the side of the shirt have busted open. Oops!

That's kind of how it is with some of the girls you hang out with, isn't it? I see you trying, trying, trying, squeezing, squeezing, squeezing to fit in with some of those girls, and it's not a great fit. Instead of trying so hard to squeeze yourself into their mold, I wish you would spend more time with the kind of girls who will help you in your walk with Me. There are some great girls wishing they had a friend like you.

Today, take some time to think about the girls in your circle of friends. Which ones aren't a good fit? Now think of some of the girls around you whom you could befriend. I promise you this: when you choose the right friends, it'll be the perfect fit—no tight squeezes!

The heartfelt counsel of a friend
is as sweet as perfume and incense.

PROVERBS 27:9 NLT

. . . .

Attention Seeking

. . . .

Sometimes you feel like you don't get enough attention from your family and friends. I know, because I can see what's inside your heart and I know when you're feeling a little sad or left out. I also see when you do things you shouldn't, just to get attention. That's never a good idea!

The next time you're worried that you're not getting enough attention, just remember that I'm always watching. I'm always listening. I'm always caring about the things that matter to you. In other words, I'm giving you lots and lots of attention, whether you notice or not. And I'm thrilled when you're doing the right things. You don't have to act up to get My attention, that's for sure!

Here's a fun idea: Instead of feeling left out, why not turn your attention to others? Look for someone else who might need a smile or someone to talk to. Then go out of your way to give that person some much-needed attention. I'll reward you when you live like that, I promise. And trust Me when I say that the people you love will reward you with kindness and attention, too.

God is not unjust; he will not forget your work and the love you have shown him as you have helped his people and continue to help them.

HEBREWS 6:10 NIV

. . . .

Perfection

. . . .

Have you ever seen the movie *Mary Poppins*?
Mary tells others that she is practically perfect
in every way. Do you think that's true? Is
anyone practically perfect in every way? I
can tell you for a fact that no one is perfect.
Well, no one but Me, anyway. There's not
one human being on earth who's reached
perfection. Everyone makes mistakes (even
Mary Poppins).

Does this mean you shouldn't try to do
your best? Of course not! Keep on trying.
You'll get better and better. Keep trying at
school. Keep trying at home. Keep trying in
your friendships. Keep trying to spend more
time with Me. Keep trying to develop your
talents and abilities. Keep working at getting
better, but don't ever get discouraged if
you think you're not perfect. I never meant
for you to be. If you were perfect, then you
wouldn't need Me.

The next time you're looking for
someone who's practically perfect in every
way, don't look in the mirror. Just look at Me.

I don't mean to say that I have already
achieved these things or that I have
already reached perfection. But I press
on to possess that perfection for which
Christ Jesus first possessed me.

PHILIPPIANS 3:12 NLT

. . . .

Bullying

Bullying is wrong. When you're the one being bullied, it's wrong. When you're the one doing the bullying, it's wrong. There's no other way to say it: it's never okay to bully someone else. When I see My kids being mean to one another, it breaks My heart.

I want you to be different, sweet girl. Don't participate in bullying, no matter how many people try to get you to do it. Don't join in. Even if the people being bullied are different from the kids you hang out with, don't use that as an excuse. No one deserves to be bullied.

Set an example for others. I'm going to give you the courage to tell an adult so that the bullying can stop. Don't be afraid. I'll go with you and help you every step of the way. Others will see that you were bold enough to do something about the bullying and will follow your lead. You can change your family, your school, even your whole community by putting a stop to bullying today.

Dear friends, never take revenge.
Leave that to the righteous anger of
God. For the Scriptures say,
"I will take revenge; I will pay them
back,' says the LORD. Instead,
"If your enemies are hungry, feed them.
If they are thirsty, give them something
to drink. In doing this, you will heap
burning coals of shame on their heads.'

ROMANS 12:19–20 NLT

Oh, That Temper!

. . . .

Whoa, girl! Don't let your temper get the best of you. I know, I know. . .you think no one notices when you reach the boiling point, but I do. I can see inside your heart and know when you're about to boil over like a teapot. Talk about losing your cool!

Instead of getting angry, take a deep breath. Spend some time with Me. I'll help you get through it without getting so angry. Submit your temper to Me, and I'll cool you down.

Wondering how you can do that? Say something like, "Jesus, please help me! I don't like losing my cool, but I just can't seem to help it! I get so mad!"

If you will tell Me the things that bug you (who you're mad at and why), I'll show you how to forgive and forget. I'll also teach you how to respond when people get you worked up. In other words, I'll put an end to that temper by cooling you down. So hang out with Me awhile. We'll pack up that temper and send it running!

Stop being angry! Turn from your rage! Do not lose your temper—it only leads to harm.

PSALM 37:8 NLT

. . . .

How Do You Measure Up?

. . . .

I see you, precious daughter. I know you're trying so hard to measure up to those around you. You see all of their good points but few of your own. So you try and try and try to get better. All of your hard work pays off, but I want you to know that you already measure up in My eyes. You don't have to work hard to impress Me. I love you to the moon and back, even on those days when you don't feel like you compare to others.

Don't worry about being "as talented as" or "as good as" the other girls. That's not the most important thing. I'm looking at your heart, and I want to make sure you realize that you're adored no matter what you do or don't do. So rest easy! Throw away that measuring stick. There's no reason to compare yourself to others. I don't see things that way. Why should you?

We do not dare to compare ourselves with those who think they are very important. They use themselves to measure themselves, and they judge themselves by what they themselves are. This shows that they know nothing.

2 CORINTHIANS 10:12 NCV

· ·

In Storage

. . . .

Have you ever seen a storage facility? It's a place where people store stuff while they're not using it. They store everything from furniture to clothing to office equipment.

When you put something in storage, it's because you don't expect to use it for a long time. There are so many things I've given you (gifts, talents, abilities) that I don't want you to store away. They're meant to be used. Oh, I know. . .you're a little shy. You don't always feel like using those gifts or letting people know that you have abilities at all. You'd rather hide your talents from others so that you're not embarrassed. But you know what? If you put them in storage, they will get dusty. If you decide to pull them out years from now (when you're older), you'll have to work harder than ever.

So don't hide those gifts away. And while you're at it, don't hide the love in your heart from others either.

I do not hide your righteousness in
my heart; I speak of your faithfulness
and your saving help. I do not conceal
your love and your faithfulness
from the great assembly.

PSALM 40:10 NIV

Busyness

. . . .

Whew! You're one busy girl. You're on the go all the time, aren't you? I see all that you're trying to do, and I also see how tired you're getting. Would you do Me a favor? Take care of yourself! I mean that. I created you to accomplish great things, but that won't happen if you don't get the rest you need.

Think about your life like a stoplight. There's green (go), red (stop), and yellow (slow down). You're at the green stage much of the time. You've been go-go-going so fast! Now it's time to put the brakes on and slow down a bit. When you see the yellow light, you know that rest is coming, and rest is a good thing!

Why do I care so much about your busy schedule? Because I see all the things you are going to accomplish in your life. Great things, girl! But the only way you'll have the energy to do everything is if you pace yourself. So get ready! Things are about to slow down.

"Come to Me, all who are weary and heavy-laden, and I will give you rest."

MATTHEW 11:28 NASB

· ·

Growing Up

· · · · · · · · · · · · · · · · ·

You're growing up! I don't know if you've noticed, but you're changing. . .a lot. Even in one year's time you've changed completely: your hair, your height, even your shoe size! And more changes are on the way. Change is part of growing.

Do you ever wonder what you're going to look like when you're grown up? I don't have to wonder. I already know. And did you ever wonder what sort of job you'll have? I know that, too! Maybe you're wondering why I don't just clue you in and tell you all of that now. I'd prefer to make it a surprise. Surprises are fun!

So don't worry about all the changes you're going through. And don't worry about the changes yet to come. Just rest easy, girl! I know how things are going to turn out, and it's going to be such fun to watch you change and grow.

"Have I not commanded you? Be strong and courageous. Do not be frightened, and do not be dismayed, for the LORD your God is with you wherever you go."

JOSHUA 1:9 ESV

Caring for Those in Need

. . . .

Did you know it makes My heart smile when I see you taking care of people in need? What a wonderful thing for you to do—to give of your own time to care for others.

Are you wondering how you can reach out to others in need? Here are some fun ideas. (Remember to ask your mom or dad to help you.) If there's an elderly person in your neighborhood, maybe you could offer to visit once a week. If someone nearby is sick, perhaps you could make a special card for them. If your best friend's mom has lost her job, perhaps your family could buy groceries for them or purchase a gift card to a local restaurant.

There are so many fun ways to care for others in need, but the very greatest thing you can possibly do is to love them and pray for them. When people know they are loved, it gives them hope, and hope is such a wonderful thing to have! So keep on giving, precious girl! Keep on caring for others. It makes Me so happy to see you giving and giving and giving. What a joy!

Do not merely look out for
your own personal interests,
but also for the interests of others.

PHILIPPIANS 2:4 NASB

. . . .

Reach the World

· · · · · · · · · · · · · · · · ·

Maybe you've read the verses in the Bible about "going into all the world to preach the Gospel" and you're confused. How can you—a young girl—go into all the world? You're not even allowed to ride your bike down the street without permission. How can you go to China, Africa, or places like that?

Here's something I want you to think about. Did you know that your "world" is the area around you? It's your neighborhood, your school, your family. Sometimes "going into all the world" is as simple as sharing your faith with a friend down the street or with a family member who doesn't believe in Me.

Sure, you'll grow up someday and maybe you really will travel to places around the world. Maybe you will take a mission trip to a third-world country or donate money so that others can do so. But in the meantime just remember this: your world is where you live. . .right now. So don't be afraid! Go on! Reach your world.

And then he told them, "Go into
all the world and preach the
Good News to everyone.'

MARK 16:15 NLT

. . . .

Stick to It

. . . .

Have you ever used a piece of double-sided tape? It's sticky on both sides, and it's really strong. In fact, it's so strong that it's hard to peel off once you've put it on. That's kind of how I want you to be once you decide to do something. Stick with it, just like that tape sticks to things.

What do I mean by that? Well, remember that time you started your homework but then didn't want to finish it? And what about that time you told your mom you would clean your room? You started, but then got distracted by a friend who wanted you to come and hang out. Oh, and remember that time you wanted to take piano lessons and it only lasted a few weeks?

The thing about sticking with something is it's not always easy. Why? Because you get bored. But if you'll stick with it, you'll break through the boredom and hit the finish line. There's nothing sweeter than finishing something you've started. It makes you feel so good!

So the next time you start something, tell yourself, "I'm going to finish this!" Then do your best to complete the task, no matter how difficult.

Now you should finish what you started.
Let the eagerness you showed in the
beginning be matched now by your giving.
Give in proportion to what you have.

2 CORINTHIANS 8:11 NLT

....

The Good Samaritan

. . . .

Have you ever read the story of the Good Samaritan? I must admit, it's one of My favorite stories in My book, the Bible. It's the story of a man who was badly injured by others and left to die on the side of the road. (Sad so far, right?) Well, just about the time he had given up hope, a man came by and helped him. The man (a Samaritan) cared for the injured man and made sure he received medical treatment. He even paid for it!

There are some wonderful people in this world, aren't there? Some people will do just about anything for others, even if it costs them money to do it. The Good Samaritan was generous and kind and went out of his way to make sure the injured man was okay. I want you to be like that. There are all sorts of people at your school and in your neighborhood who are hurting. Oh, they might not be injured, but maybe their feelings are hurt or they're feeling left out. You can be like the Samaritan and help that person feel loved and cared for once again. Sure, you might have to go out of your way, but you'll feel good when you share My love with others, I promise!

"But a Samaritan, as he traveled,
came where the man was; and when
he saw him, he took pity on him."

LUKE 10:33 NIV

. . . .

Goals

. . . .

Do you know what it means to set goals? A goal is more than a dream, it's something you can actually achieve if you set your mind to it.

Here's an example. Imagine you wanted to run in a long race—three miles—but you weren't a very strong runner. You would begin to prepare for the race months ahead of time, running, running, running and getting stronger, stronger, stronger. When you first started training, you could barely run a half mile. Then, after a while, you could run a full mile. Then two. And then finally, three miles! By the time the race day arrived, you made it to your final goal (the finish line) because you practiced, practiced, practiced!

The same is true in your relationship with Me. You can set goals for prayer time, Bible study, and even scripture memory. Start small so you don't get overwhelmed. Before long you'll be a superstar able to memorize line after line.

Go ahead. . .set small goals. Soon you'll be achieving big things.

But the plans of the LORD stand firm forever, the purposes of his heart through all generations.

PSALM 33:11 NIV

· ·

Fear

. . . .

It's no fun to be fearful, is it? I see you when you're afraid. Your knees shake and your voice trembles! You're scared from the inside out. But you don't have to be afraid. You really don't. I'm your protector, the One who's always looking out for you. No matter what you go through, you're not alone. And guess what? I have angels looking out for you, too. You're surrounded by them.

The next time you start to get scared, just think of Me standing right there next to you holding your hand. Then envision those angels, big and bold, standing between you and the thing you're scared of. One word from Me and fear has to go! (It's true! My Word tells you that even the demons tremble when they hear the name of Jesus!)

So speak My name. Speak it loud and clear. Tell that fear to skedaddle in the name of Jesus, then watch as it disappears!

So do not fear, for I am with you;
do not be dismayed, for I am your God.
I will strengthen you and help you;
I will uphold you with my
righteous right hand.

ISAIAH 41:10 NIV

· ·

Keep Your Eyes on Me

. . . .

Remember that time you went to the swimming pool and your eyes were really blurry afterward? Blurry vision is no fun! Everyone wants to be able to see clearly at all times. When you can't see where you're going, you bump into things. *Bam! Crash! Pow!*

Would you like to know a little secret? The very best way to have good vision is to keep your eyes on Me. Oh, I know, I know. . .you can't really see Me with your eyes. But you can see Me with your heart. And you can follow the words in My book, the Bible. Those words will give you the clearest vision ever!

Not sure how that works? Imagine you're going through a really hard time and you have some big decisions to make. You worry and worry because you don't know how it's going to turn out. Then you open your Bible and read a verse that gives you great direction. After reading the verse you suddenly know which way to go, which decision to make. You realize that everything is going to work out just fine.

My Word helps you keep your focus on Me, and I love it when you're looking My way. Why? Because I adore you and want to spend time showing you a better way to live. So focus, sweet girl! There! That makes everything better.

Keep your eyes on Jesus, who both began and finished this race we're in. Study how he did it. Because he never lost sight of where he was headed—that exhilarating finish in and with God—he could put up with anything along the way: Cross, shame, whatever. And now he's there, in the place of honor, right alongside God.

HEBREWS 12:2 MSG

Run the Race

. . . .

Life is kind of like a race. You run and run, then get tired and want to stop. I want you to make it all the way to the finish line, so I'm going to give you some pointers that will help.

The next time you're weary, think about Moses who led the Israelites to the Promised Land. They traveled for years to get to their destination!

The next time you think about quitting, remember Jonah. He tried to quit too, but I wouldn't let him.

The next time you're wondering if you have the strength to face your enemies, remember David who used a slingshot and a handful of stones to defeat a giant.

The next time you say, "I'm just a kid!" remember Timothy, one of My greatest disciples. I had to remind him that being young wasn't a problem.

All of the great people who've ever run My race have faced obstacles, but all of them were overcomers. You'll be an overcomer too, if you just follow the example of the runners you read about in My Word. So what's keeping you? Grab your Bible and start reading!

Therefore, since we are surrounded
by such a great cloud of witnesses,
let us throw off everything that hinders
and the sin that so easily entangles.
And let us run with perseverance the
race marked out for us, fixing our eyes on
Jesus, the pioneer and perfecter of faith.

HEBREWS 12:1–2 NIV

. . . .

Consequences

. . . .

Actions have consequences. I know you've already experienced a few of those. Remember that time you lied to your mom and got caught in the lie? What happened? You were disciplined. And remember that time you ate too much sugar and got sick to your stomach? Consequences.

You might wonder why I decided that consequences are a good idea. They're a great teacher! Think of it this way: maybe your mom tells you to bring her your dirty clothes so she can put them in the washer. You forget, so the clothes never get washed. Then when you need clothes for school the next day, nothing is clean! You have nothing to wear. You end up wearing dirty jeans and a wrinkled, smelly T-shirt to school. Because you didn't do the right thing (give the dirty clothes to your mom to wash), you had consequences (no clean clothes).

It's always important to do the right thing. . .right away. And don't just do it because you're worried about getting in trouble. Do the right thing because it's the right thing to do. Your good behavior makes My heart happy, and guess what? Good behavior has good consequences! Now that's a lovely idea!

For whoever keeps the whole law
but fails in one point has become
accountable for all of it.

JAMES 2:10 ESV

. . . .

Idols

. . . .

What does it mean to have idols? When you "idolize" something, it means you make it more important than Me. Want an example? Imagine it's almost your birthday. You've been hoping and praying your parents get you a certain present. It's all you can think or talk about. The big day arrives and. . .yay! You get the special item. It's just as wonderful as you thought it would be. You love it and take it everywhere with you. It's a part of you. You couldn't possibly live without it.

Maybe that's kind of a silly example, but I see things like this happen all the time. You wouldn't believe the things My kids idolize: TV stars, famous singers, video games. . .you name it! I keep trying to remind them they need to put Me first, but many keep forgetting.

Don't be like the ones who forget. I want to take first place in your life. Don't put Me at the end of the line. Put Me at the front, okay? Nothing can take My place, after all!

"You shall not make for yourself an
idol, or any likeness of what is in
heaven above or on the earth beneath
or in the water under the earth."

EXODUS 20:4 NASB

. . . .

Caring for the Elderly

. . . .

I want you to respect and admire older people. Why? Because they're My kids too, even though they're much older than you. Sure, they don't look like kids, but they are!

Some girls don't like to hang out with older people. They don't think they have much in common with them. But this breaks My heart. I want you to care for people who are elderly. How can you care for them, you ask? Why not visit with an elderly neighbor? Bake her some cookies or write her a sweet note. Ask your parents or your Sunday school teacher to take you on an outing to a nursing home. Perhaps you and your friends can put together a little choir and sing to them or take board games to play.

The point is, elderly people—no matter where they live—love to spend time with kids. They do! They enjoy telling stories and singing songs. They love eating cookies and making people laugh. So don't be afraid to hang out with someone who's much older. You'll learn a lot, and you'll make My heart happy, too!

"I will be your God throughout your
lifetime—until your hair is white with age.
I made you, and I will care for you.
I will carry you along and save you."

ISAIAH 46:4 NLT

. . . .

Well Designed

. . . .

Have you ever taken the time to look at the house you live in? Do you see how it's made? The walls are in a certain place. So are the ceilings. Everything is just where it should be.

What if the bathroom was in the kitchen or the bedroom in the hallway? That wouldn't make much sense, would it? No! Everything is in its rightful place because the designer, the one who came up with the plan for the house, knew what she was doing! She created the perfect plan with all of the rooms in just the right place.

Did you know that your body is like a house? It's true! And all of the rooms (your heart, your mind, your soul) are designed by Yours Truly (Me—Jesus!). I'm a really great designer. I created your eyes, your hair, your skin, your fingernails. . .everything. And if you think the outside of your body is amazing, you should see what's going on in the inside. Wow! What's happening in your heart is pretty remarkable! And your lungs. And your brain. I took great care in designing every one of those things. You are more brilliantly constructed than the greatest computer, and you are destined to do great things for Me.

For you created my inmost being;
you knit me together in my mother's womb.
I praise you because I am fearfully
and wonderfully made; your works are
wonderful, I know that full well.

PSALM 139:13–14 NIV

....

Ears to Hear

. . . .

Sometimes you tune out what others are saying. I know this because there have been times I've whispered words to your heart and you've ignored them. I've also seen a few times when you've tuned out your parents or grandparents. They say, "Go do your homework," and you pretend you didn't hear. Or they give you instructions to clean out your closet, and you act like you didn't really hear them. Admit it! You know it's true.

Sometimes you choose not to hear because you don't want to obey. This is never good! Listening to your parents is critical! They're loaded with good advice. And guess what? Hearing My voice is even more critical because I'm always giving you good advice and instruction. And you need instruction sometimes! So when you hear My still, small voice, just say, "I'm listening, Lord." Than lean in close so that you can hear. You don't want to miss a word. What I have to say might just change your life!

"He who has ears to hear,
let him hear."

MATTHEW 11:15 ESV

. . . .

Speak the Truth!

. . . .

I'm a truth-lover. It really hurts My heart when My girls lie. Oh, I know, I know. . .you think you don't lie. But is this really the case? Remember that time your mom asked who broke her glass plate? You acted like you didn't know, but you're the one who did it. And remember that time when your teacher asked everyone to raise their hand if they finished their homework? You raised your hand, but you hadn't exactly finished every bit of it.

Here's the thing: honesty is hard sometimes, but it's always the right thing to do. When your mom asked about the plate, saying the words, "I'm so sorry, Mom, but I accidentally broke it," might've been hard, but your mom would have forgiven you for breaking her plate. And instead of lying to your teacher, what if you'd told her the truth: "I'm sorry, Mrs. Baker, but I fell asleep last night before finishing my homework." Chances are, the teacher might just give you a second chance. Maybe.

The point is, you can be a truth-teller, even when it's really hard. I'm so grateful for My truth-telling girls!

"My words come from
an upright heart; my lips
sincerely speak what I know."

JOB 33:3 NIV

· ·

Authority

· · · · · · · · · · · · · · · · · ·

Maybe you've heard other kids say, "You're not the boss of me!" Maybe you've even said those words yourself! Truth is, no one wants to be bossed around, no matter how old they are. A true leader doesn't boss people around. A real leader (person in charge) leads with a gentle spirit.

Have you ever wondered who the real boss is? I'm the ultimate Boss, but I have placed others in your life, too: your parents, your teachers, people at church who teach your classes, and so on. These special people aren't there to "boss you around." They're there to lead and guide you and show you the way to go. Why? So that you can have boundaries and be safe! These people are called "authority" (experts), and they guide you because they adore you!

Today, think about all the authority figures in your life: mom, dad, grandparents, friends' parents, teachers, and so on. How can you treat them with respect? By doing what they ask when they ask it. By saying please and thank you. By obeying, even when it's really hard. Submitting yourself to authority is My plan for a happy life. So don't worry about anyone trying to be the boss of you. They're simply there to lead and guide you because they love you. And the kindest thing you can do in response is to love them back by obeying.

Let every person be subject to the governing authorities. For there is no authority except from God, and those that exist have been instituted by God.

ROMANS 13:1 ESV

Extraordinary

. . . .

Do you know what it means to be extra-ordinary? Look at the word *ordinary* for a moment. No one wants to be ordinary, do they? To be ordinary means you're plain. Average. Most girls want to be *extra*-ordinary. Above and beyond! They want to be girls people will remember because of the amazing way they lived their lives!

How can you be extraordinary? You can set an example for others with your great behavior. One of the finest ways to live an extraordinary life is by surprising people with kind gestures. . .for no reason. There's a lot of fun ways to bless others with little surprises. Writing a kind note. Preparing a meal. Setting the table for Mom. There are a thousand ways to live an extraordinary life. Be the best student you can be. Be the best daughter, the best friend, the best neighbor.

Today, think of three ways you can be extraordinary. Write them down and then do your best to have an extraordinary day!

Because we know that this extraordinary
day is just ahead, we pray for you
all the time—pray that our God will
make you fit for what he's called you to
be, pray that he'll fill your good ideas
and acts of faith with his own energy so
that it all amounts to something.
If your life honors the name of Jesus,
he will honor you. Grace is behind and
through all of this, our God giving
himself freely, the Master,
Jesus Christ, giving himself freely.

2 THESSALONIANS 1:11–12 MSG

Abilities

· · · · · · · · · · · · · · · · · · ·

Have you ever looked at the word *abilities* and wondered what it meant? To have an ability means you're able to do something. Some people are doctors and nurses. They're able to take care of the sick. Others are teachers. They're able to share the gift of knowledge. Still others are musicians. They bless people with their songs.

Where do these abilities come from? Do these people just work hard until they're finally able? They do put in a lot of work, for sure, but they still couldn't accomplish much without My help. I give them the desire to want to do great things, and then I help them every step of the way.

I'm helping you, too! Did you know that I've placed abilities inside of you, precious daughter? I have! You are able to do many, many things. And as you grow, so will your abilities. By the time you're a woman, you will be able to do things that you can't even dream of now. So hang on for the ride! The road has lots of opportunities ahead.

Now, dear brothers and sisters,
regarding your question about the
special abilities the Spirit gives us.
I don't want you to misunderstand this.

1 CORINTHIANS 12:1 NLT

. . . .

Death

. . . .

I know that a lot of girls hear the word *death* and get scared. Really, really scared. One of the reasons people are so scared of death is because they don't know what happens on the other side of it. But you know what, precious daughter? You don't have to worry. . .at all! Nope. Want to know why? Because everyone who puts their trust in Me and accepts Me as Lord and Savior gets to come to heaven to live with Me after they die.

If you think about it, death is like a river. You have to drive over a bridge to get to the other side of the river. When Christians die, they cross over the bridge to heaven, a wonderful place, unlike anything you've ever experienced on earth. I promise, it's better than any vacation you've ever been on or any amusement park you've ever visited! In heaven no one ever has any pain or sickness. And in heaven everyone lives forever. Wow!

So please don't worry if someone you know and love passes away. It's okay to miss them, of course. I would be concerned if you didn't get sad! But please don't grieve forever. Instead, look forward to the day when you see that person again in heaven.

You'll have the time of your life there and you won't ever have to worry about death again.

"He will wipe away every tear from their eyes, and there will be no more death, sadness, crying, or pain, because all the old ways are gone.'

REVELATION 21:4 NCV

· ·

Learning Curve

. . . .

Have you ever wondered how the really talented singers—the ones on the radio or TV—get so good? Do you think they always sounded like that? The truth is, they had to learn. . .just like you. Everyone is on a learning curve, you know.

Oh, you don't know what a learning curve is? Well, let Me explain. It's like a long, curved road. On one end stands you, the person with a lot to learn. The other end of the road is where you will eventually end up, but first you have to get past the big curve in the middle. Only one problem: it's a l-o-n-g curve that will take a l-o-n-g time to get around. Oh, but it's a learning curve! If you'll stay on the road, you'll learn all you need to know to get to the other side, and once you get there, you'll be much wiser than you are today.

Where are you on the learning curve, sweet girl? Are you still willing to learn? Still willing to keep going, even when you are discouraged? Just think about those people on the radio. They were on a learning curve. . .and they stuck to it!

A wise man will hear and increase
in learning, and a man of
understanding will acquire wise counsel.

PROVERBS 1:5 NASB

. . . .

Miracles Still Happen

. . . .

I see how it is. You hear the stories in the Bible about the miracles I performed and you wonder if I still do stuff like that. You ask yourself, "Does God still heal people today?" or "Will God provide for my family like He did for the people in the Bible?" You even ask yourself, "Does God love me like He loved David? If so, will He help me slay giants?"

The answer is yes! Miracles aren't just something you read about in the Bible. They're happening all around you! Remember that time you scraped your knee and it healed up over time? That was a miracle! I created your body in a miraculous way, to heal itself! Oh, and remember that one Christmas when your dad was out of work and Christmas presents miraculously appeared on your front porch? I was the One behind that, too.

Yes, miracles are happening every day: when a baby is born, when someone gets a new job, whenever My kids call on Me. I love to do the miraculous. . .just wait and see!

The waters were divided, and the Israelites went through the sea on dry ground, with a wall of water on their right and on their left.

EXODUS 14:21–22 NIV

. . . .

Nature

. . . .

I have a fun idea. As soon as you're able, why not step outside and take a look around. Oh, I know. . .you go outside all the time to play and hang out with your friends. But instead of doing that, just stop and look around you. See that butterfly with its gorgeous colors and delicate wings? I made that! Look at that huge oak tree with leaves changing colors right before your eyes. I designed it that way. And those clouds! Aren't they the perfect color of white up against a beautiful blue sky? I thought so, too!

All of creation is My design. I could've made the grass purple and the sky yellow, but that didn't seem right to Me. I could've made tree lizards blue and bananas gray, but that didn't seem right, either. Instead, I created everything just as it is for your viewing pleasure. My creation is like a great artistic masterpiece: beautiful to look at and marvelous to enjoy.

So the next time you go outside, take a moment to look around. Enjoy the breeze. Smile when you see the birds flying overhead. Giggle as the grass tickles your toes. Have fun in My creation. I made it all just for you!

Let the skies rejoice and the earth be glad; let the sea and everything in it shout. Let the fields and everything in them rejoice. Then all the trees of the forest will sing for joy.

PSALM 96:11–12 NCV

Hide-and-Seek

. . . .

Peekaboo, I see you!

Oh, I know. . .you're trying to hide from Me because you feel ashamed of something you did, but you don't have to hide. You don't even have to be ashamed. Whenever you do something wrong, all you have to do is ask for My forgiveness and I will forgive you, no problem! So pull those hands down, girl! Don't cover your eyes and face, even if you're feeling very, very ashamed of what you've done. Instead, look My way without worrying that I will be angry. You will find that My eyes are filled with love for you, no matter what you've done.

Why don't I like to play hide-and-seek? Because I don't ever want you to be afraid to just come to Me and tell Me what you're struggling with. Don't worry. I won't be mad at you or stop loving you. In fact, it makes My heart very, very happy when you admit you've done something wrong. Hiding it and hoping no one finds out makes Me very sad!

So no hiding, sweet girl!

"Can anyone hide from me in a secret place? Am I not everywhere in all the heavens and earth?' says the LORD.

JEREMIAH 23:24 NLT

. . . .

Cleanliness

. . . .

I see how cluttered your room gets sometimes. I can hardly see the floor! Taking care of your stuff is really important, but sometimes you fall down on the job. And speaking of falling down, with all that stuff on the floor, someone is going to trip and fall! Better pick it up before a catastrophe strikes!

Remember that scene in *Mary Poppins* where she snapped her fingers and the room started cleaning itself? Don't you wish life was like that? How wonderful would it be to watch your room get itself in perfect order. (Ah, what a lovely dream!)

Unfortunately, there are no buttons to push. As your mama likes to say, "You made the mess, and you have to clean it up." Mama's right, by the way! It's only fair for the person who made the mess to clean it up.

It's time to tidy up, girl! Pick up those toys. Make that bed. Get those clothes picked up. Dust those cobwebs out of the corners. When your room is spick-and-span, you'll feel so much better, and you'll even be able to see the floor!

"Wash yourselves; make yourselves clean; remove the evil of your deeds from before my eyes; cease to do evil."

ISAIAH 1:16 ESV

. . . .

Siblings

. . . .

Did you know that I designed each family?
I chose the brothers and sisters who would
live together in one house. I handpicked
each brother, sister, mother, father,
grandmother, cousin, uncle, aunt, and so on.
I know you're not all alike, but that's what
makes life fun! I designed families to have
different types of people in them.

All right, all right. . .I know what you're
thinking. (I really do!) You're thinking, *My
brother is* too *different. He doesn't even like
me.* It probably seems like that, but I happen
to know he loves you, in spite of how he
acts. I also know it's not always easy to get
along. Sometimes I see you fighting and I
want to tap you on the shoulder and say,
"Hey! Just a little reminder! You need to be
getting along down there."

So what do you do if you have brothers
and sisters who don't get along? You don't stir
up trouble. You learn to forgive and forget.
You have to remember that love is the glue
that fixes every broken relationship. In the
meantime, enjoy your family members and
don't forget to pray for them. They need it!

Keep on loving one another
as brothers and sisters.

HEBREWS 13:1 NIV

. . . .

Thirsty for Me

. . . .

Imagine you're walking in the desert and have no water to drink. You're parched and dry. Oh, how you would love a giant glass of water. You would do almost anything for just one sip! That feeling of thirst is natural. I gave it to you so that you would remember to keep your body hydrated and healthy. If you weren't ever thirsty, you would never remember to drink!

Did you know that I also designed you to be thirsty for Me? It's true. But what does that mean? How can a person be thirsty for God? Am I like a drink of water?

In many ways, I *am* like a drink of water! I can satisfy you when you're going through a hard, dry time. Maybe you're feeling lonely or afraid and you decide to pray. (Those feelings of loneliness are like thirst! Those feelings make you want to spend time with Me.) When you come to Me in prayer, I pour out My love (much like water is poured out). Before long, you're feeling better.

Stay thirsty, girl! Drink plenty of real water and come to Me for living water, too. What's living water? It's the kind of water I give to those who ask. . .the kind that never runs dry.

"Whoever believes in me, as Scripture
has said, rivers of living water
will flow from within them.'

JOHN 7:38 NIV

· ·

My Promises

. . . .

I know you get tired of broken promises. It's so discouraging when people say they're going to do something and then don't follow through. It's also a real bummer when people say they're going to stick with you— be your friend for life—and then forget all about you and start hanging out with other people instead.

I see the pain that broken promises cause you, sweet girl, and it breaks My heart. But I want you to know something amazing: I'm a promise-keeper, not a promise-breaker.

How can you learn from My example? Be a girl who follows through. To follow through means you don't just say it—you *do* it. And you don't just do it part of the way. You complete the task. Why? Because you promised you would.

It feels so good to fulfill your promises. And you know what? People are watching and learning from your example. Before long, they will become promise-keepers, too!

He did not waver at the promise of God through unbelief, but was strengthened in faith, giving glory to God.

ROMANS 4:20 NKJV

. . . .

Listen Up!

. . . .

Sometimes your ears get filled with wax.
They need to be cleaned out. (Icky!) And
sometimes you put your fingers in your ears
just to drown out the sounds around you. I
understand. Life is noisy! Some people wear
earplugs just to muffle the noise.

So how do you hear My voice if your ears
are plugged? Do you hear with your actual
ears? Here's a little secret: everyone can hear
My voice, even people who are completely
deaf and have no hearing in their ears at all.
How is this possible? Because you hear Me
with your heart and your spirit, not your ears.

I'm always speaking to My kids. If you're
listening with your heart, you'll hear Me say,
"Good morning! Welcome to a new day!
Why don't you come and meet with Me?"
I also love to whisper things like, "Calm
down! Don't get so mad at your mom when
she tells you to do something." Sometimes
I even lean in close to tell you things like, "I
love you, sweet girl, even when you feel like
no one else does."

Yes, I'm always speaking to your heart,
so listen up! Maybe, just maybe, you'll hear
something that will change your life.

"If only you listen obediently to the voice of the LORD your God, to observe carefully all this commandment which I am commanding you today.'

DEUTERONOMY 15:5 NASB

The Golden Rule

. . . .

I see how it is. Sometimes you argue and fight with your brothers and sisters over the silliest things! You want the biggest half of the cheeseburger. You want the largest ice-cream cone. You want more of your parents' attention. You want to go shopping with Mom by yourself while the other kids stay home. When you don't get what you want, you get upset with those around you and you argue or cry. Most of the time this happens because you're jealous.

What if you changed your attitude? What if you started wishing for others to have the bigger bowl of ice cream and the most attention? Could you really learn to be happy if others got the yummiest piece of pie or got to go to the store with Mom instead of you? It's hard, but this is how I want you to live.

Life is filled with opportunities to wish the best for others. And I like this! I want My kids to treat others the way they want to be treated. If you want more love, show others more love. If you want more joy, then live more joyfully. Do you need more attention from Mom? Then show her more attention. Surprise her with little gifts and love notes.

"Do unto others." It's a great way to live, girl!

"Do to others as you
would have them do to you."

LUKE 6:31 NIV

. . . .

Insecurity

. . . .

I knew you before you were born. And I created you just like you are. Those freckles? They were My idea! Those curls? Yep, My idea, too! I knew just what you would look like, and I want you to be happy with that. I want you to be happy with your gifts and abilities, too. So don't compare yourself to others. Maybe someone else can sing or dance better than you, but that's okay.

Sometimes when you're insecure you feel alone, but guess what? You wouldn't believe how many of your friends tell Me the same thing. It's true! That girl who sits across from you at the lunch table? She gets insecure sometimes. And that girl at recess, the one who's always bossing people around? She does that because she doesn't feel very confident. So many of My girls struggle with this, so just know. . .you're not alone.

I want you to be strong and confident. You can learn to love and appreciate the way I designed you. To Me, you're the most beautiful girl in the world. And you're perfect just as you are.

*You are altogether beautiful,
my love; there is no flaw in you.*

SONG OF SOLOMON 4:7 ESV

. . . .

Apologies

The words "I'm sorry" are the hardest two words to speak. Saying you're sorry means you were wrong. Who wants to be wrong? No one. But sometimes you make mistakes. You hurt people, or you hurt their feelings. When those times come, it's always best to get those two hard words behind you. Say "I'm sorry" right away. . .and mean it. Don't just mumble the words because Mom says you have to. Mean them in your heart because I'm watching and I know when you're being honest.

I know! Sometimes other people should apologize to you. . .but they don't. I'm working on their hearts, too. So don't get mad if someone refuses to apologize or won't admit they did something wrong. Instead, just forgive them and allow Me to do the work inside their heart.

Why do I feel so strongly about apologies? Because I'm all about forgiveness. I want people to live in peace with one another and get along. That's how I designed you to be. So admit when you're wrong, then watch as I make everything right again.

For godly grief produces a repentance
that leads to salvation without regret,
whereas worldly grief produces death.
2 CORINTHIANS 7:10 ESV

. . . .

Feelings

. . . .

I know all about feelings. I created them, after all. I can see straight into your heart, so I know when you're happy, when you're sad, and even when you get angry. There's nothing wrong with feelings, but you can't let them control you.

Need an example? Think of a puppet on a string. The puppet only does what the puppeteer allows it to do. Some people are like that. They let their feelings control them just like a puppeteer controls a puppet with those strings. Here's the problem, though. Sometimes you have rough days and those strings get all twisted around. Your feelings go a little crazy. You can't seem to control them.

It's time to cut the strings. You can do that by asking for My help. I don't mind if you spend a little time crying, but if your emotions get the best of you, it can ruin your whole day and I surely don't want that. What are you waiting for? Call on Me and I'll help you with those feelings, I promise!

And whatever you do, in word or deed, do everything in the name of the Lord Jesus, giving thanks to God the Father through him.

COLOSSIANS 3:17 ESV

. . . .

Heroes

· · · · · · · · · · · · · · · · ·

Who is your hero? Many of My girls would name a superhero like Wonder Woman. But I'm talking about real-life heroes, the people you admire or the people who work hard to make your life easier. Who are some of the people who have cared for you and helped you through hard times? Who are some of the people in your community who make life easier (and safer) for others? You are surrounded by heroes every day.

It's time to honor these amazing people! Do something special for the heroes in your life. Choose one person today: Your mother. Your teacher. A firefighter. A police officer. The postal worker who delivers your mail.

And while you're at it, why not become a hero to others? Want to know how you can do that? Take a look at the verse below. If you're quick to listen, slow to speak, and slow to anger, you will be admired by others. It's true. So don't just celebrate the heroes in your life today. Become a hero!

Know this, my beloved brothers:
let every person be quick to hear,
slow to speak, slow to anger;
for the anger of man does not
produce the righteousness of God.

JAMES 1:19–20 ESV

My Valentine

Have you ever made valentines for those you love? A valentine is a lovely way to show someone that you care, especially if you make the card yourself and write a sweet note inside.

Did you know that I've written a special valentine just for you? It's called the Bible. Inside of that wonderful book, I've written down special love messages for you that will make your heart so happy! Why did I take the time to give you My Word? Because I adore you! I want you to see how much you are loved.

If you search really, really deep in My Valentine, the Bible, you'll find that I don't just love you—I love everyone. . .even the most unlovable person on the earth. How is that possible, you ask? My love is deeper than any river and higher than any mountain. It goes w-a-y above anything you've ever felt in your heart. (Can you imagine?)

Today, please celebrate My Valentine by sharing it with others. Tell your friends about My Word, My valentine to them. Everyone needs a little more love!

"The LORD appeared to him from far away. I have loved you with an everlasting love; therefore I have continued my faithfulness to you."

JEREMIAH 31:3 ESV

. . . .

Division

. . . .

Have you ever heard the word *division*? Maybe you've studied division in math class. Here's a math problem to refresh your memory: If you had eight apples and divided that number in half, how many apples would you have? Four, right?

When it comes to math problems, division is a good thing. But when it comes to relationships, it's never good. Want an example? Let's say you're good friends with five girls. Five plus one (you!) equals six. Then one of the girls gets into an argument with another, and before you know it, the group has divided. Three girls in one group. Three in another. And everyone starts to gossip, which only divides people even more.

Would you like to know why I don't like this kind of division? Because I'm all about unity. When you walk in unity with one another, it means you're a team. You stick together. When you divide, it breaks My heart. So no division! Let's keep this team together, shall we?

I appeal to you, brothers, by the name of our Lord Jesus Christ, that all of you agree, and that there be no divisions among you, but that you be united in the same mind and the same judgment.

1 CORINTHIANS 1:10–13 ESV

Being a Good Neighbor

. . . .

I want all of My kids to be great neighbors. Maybe you read that and think, *I am a good neighbor! I get along with the people in my neighborhood.* The thing is, there's actually more to it than that. A "neighbor" isn't just someone who lives in a house near you. Your neighbors might live far, far away (all the way across the globe, even).

How is it possible to be neighborly to people who live far away? You can love them as you love yourself. You guard what you say (and what you think in your heart) about people who are different from you (different races, different colors, different clothing styles). In other words, you don't discriminate. You can help those in need by giving to mission organizations.

The very best way to be a good neighbor is to pray. Pray for the children in Africa. Pray for the children in the Middle East. They really, really need your prayers. Lift up special prayers for children across the globe who are dealing with poverty and sickness. When you take the time to pray, it shows Me just how much you care.

Tell every nation on earth,
"The LORD is wonderful and
does marvelous things!"

PSALM 96:3 CEV

....

My Love

· · · · · · · · · · · · · · · · ·

No one loves you like I do. Sure, your family loves you. Your grandparents or other relatives love you. Maybe you have friends who love you. But none of them—not even the person who loves you the most—loves you as much as I do. I loved you so much that I was willing to come to earth as a baby, then grow up and die on the cross for your sins.

Why would I do that? Why would I leave heaven? (It's pretty amazing up here, after all!) Why would I leave streets of gold and gates made out of pearls to come to be born in a dirty, smelly stable? I wanted you to see just how much I love you, that's why. I gave up everything to spend some time with you and to show you how to live.

My love is also written down in My book, the Bible. If you're ever feeling unloved, just pick up the Bible and read verses like the one below. You'll be reminded right away of just how loved you are. I hope that news will make your day!

How great is God's love for all
who worship him? Greater than the
distance between heaven and earth!

PSALM 103:11 CEV

. . . .

Order Out of Chaos

. . . .

Have you ever had one of those days when your mom said, "You stay in your room and clean it until it's completely done!" Maybe you worked for hours and finally (finally!) got it into shape.

That's kind of what it's like when I get involved in your life. I can take a messy situation (much like your messy room) and clean it up again.

Need an example? Imagine your best friend's parents are going through a divorce. You feel so bad for your friend. She cries and cries. To make matters worse, it's the holidays and nothing is working out for them. So you and your parents decide to invite them over to your house for Christmas dinner. Before long, you're all laughing and smiling and your friend has almost forgotten about the pain. By including them in your holiday meal, you helped them forget about the chaos and enjoy a day when everything felt good again.

I love bringing order out of chaos, and I love using My kids (like you) to help. So be on the lookout for people who are going through tough stuff. I just might use you to turn their situation around!

For He spoke, and it was done;
He commanded, and it stood fast.

PSALM 33:9 NASB

. . . .

My Plan

. . . .

Did you know that I have a plan for your life? It's a step-by-step plan, too! That means you have to move from A to B to C and so on. I know, I know. . .you wish you could skip a few steps and go right to the good stuff, but I have great things for you at every stop on the journey.

Not sure what I mean by that? Imagine you want to be a doctor when you grow up. First (A), you have to go to school and make good grades. Second (B), you have to make good choices so that you can get into a good college. Third (C), you probably have to give up time with your friends so that you can study more. Fourth (D), you have to work, work, work in the hospital as you study. Next (E, F, G. . .all the way to Z), you have to continue to work hard.

I know, I know. . .you have your own plans. And you're hoping you get your way. But I want to clue you in so that you know something very important: My plans for you are much bigger and much greater than anything you could ever dream up. So trust Me, okay? I promise. . .My plans are the best!

Many are the plans in the mind
of a man, but it is the purpose
of the LORD that will stand.

PROVERBS 19:21 ESV

Grumbling

· · · · · · · · · · · · · · · · ·

I hear you grumbling, girl! Oh, you think no one hears you because you do it under your breath, but I notice. I hear all of those things you say when you're sure no one is listening. You complain. . .a lot! And complaining always comes from a bitter heart.

I'm not a big fan of grumbling and complaining. I'd rather hear rejoicing and praise. I'd rather see you focusing on the needs of others than fretting over all the things you think you deserve.

The only way to stop grumbling is to live a life of gratitude. Look around you, at all the things you already have: a warm bed to sleep in at night. Food on the table. A family to surround you. Running water in the faucets. Friends. I've given you so much, and you need to be grateful. So before you start grumbling, spend at least five minutes praising Me for what you already have. Then I feel sure you won't even feel like grumbling at all. You'll be so grateful that you'll forget what you were grumbling about!

Do all things without grumbling or disputing.

PHILIPPIANS 2:14 ESV

. . . .

Your Provider

Maybe you've heard people say, "God is our provider," but you don't know what that means. Maybe you're wondering what exactly I provide. I could give you a long list if you like, but I'll start with the most basic things. I provide food for your tummy, water to keep you hydrated. I provide a place for you to live and the clothes you wear. I provide people to care for your needs and teachers to instruct you.

But I provide a lot more than that, too! I give you peace when you're troubled. I give you joy when you're sad. I give you friends when you're lonely. I give you strength when you're feeling weak.

Most of those things I just listed can't be purchased in a store. You can't go into the grocery store and say, "I'll have a bag of peace, please!" But you can come straight to Me and I'll give it to you at no cost whatsoever. I love to provide for My kids. It brings great joy to My heart, in fact. So whatever you're lacking. . .just ask!

And my God will supply every
need of yours according to his
riches in glory in Christ Jesus.

PHILIPPIANS 4:19 ESV

. . . .

A City on a Hill

. . . .

Sweet girl, did you know that you are a city on a hill? I know! I can see you scratching your head as you try to figure that one out. How can a girl be a city? Trust Me, it's possible!

A city on a hill is visible to everyone below. People look up at night to see the lights twinkling in all the windows. That city shines, shines, shines for all to see. That's how you are! Your faith is like a bright light. You shine for all of your friends and family members to see.

How do you shine your light? By treating others kindly when you feel like being ugly instead. By taking care of people in need, even when you're going through hard stuff yourself. By loving people unconditionally, even those who are hard to love.

Yes, indeed. You're a city on a hill, one that cannot be hidden, and you're shining bright. That makes My heart very, very happy!

"You are the light of the
world. A town built on a
hill cannot be hidden.'

MATTHEW 5:14 NIV

· ·

Eat Your Vegetables

· · · · · · · · · · · · · · · · · · ·

Not everyone likes veggies, but they're so good for you! I know, you'd rather eat french fries and chocolate milk shakes. You'd rather have candy and ice cream. But guess what? If you ate nothing but junk food all day long, you would get sick! Before long, you wouldn't want any sweets at all.

Veggies are loaded with vitamins. I made sure the soil they grew in was filled with good nutrients so that you could be healthy and strong. And that's what I want you to be—healthy and strong. Why? Because I love you, of course, and because I have a lot for you to do. You're going to need to be strong to accomplish all the great things I have for you.

What great things? Well, that's part of the adventure. You don't know what's coming during the next few years, but I sure do! That's why it's important to take care of yourself so that you're ready when the time comes. So eat your veggies. Toss that milk shake! Take care of yourself so that you can grow up to be a healthy, strong girl, ready to work for Me.

The wise store up choice food and
olive oil, but fools gulp theirs down.

PROVERBS 21:20 NIV

· ·

Following Me

. . . .

What does it mean to follow Me? Does it mean you have to leave your home, your parents, your brothers and sisters, and follow Me to places across the globe? Not at all! To follow Me means that you follow the things you learn in My Word. For example, if you have a hard choice to make, you can read the Bible and find a helpful scripture on the subject. Having a hard time in a relationship? You can follow Me by looking up verses about friendship.

Following Me also means that you treat others the way I would treat them. Whenever you're in a situation where people are getting on your nerves, just ask the question, "What would Jesus do?" If you close your eyes and listen, I'll tell you! Most of the time I just want you to forgive and treat others the way you want to be treated.

The very best way to follow Me is to spend time in My presence. I'm not saying you come to an actual "place" where I am. I'm just saying that we can meet wherever you happen to be: in your bed, in the backyard, in the living room. I'm everywhere, you know!

So follow Me, sweet girl—by reading My Word, listening to My voice, and spending time with Me.

Then Jesus said to His disciples, "If anyone wishes to come after Me, he must deny himself, and take up his cross and follow Me."

MATTHEW 16:24 NASB

A Sweet-Smelling Girl

. . . .

Mmm. Don't you love yummy smells? I created flowers with the loveliest aromas. And what about the smell of cookies baking in the oven? You can hardly wait to eat them because they smell so good. And popcorn! Don't you just love the smell of popcorn popping? It's the first thing you want to eat when you go to the movies, and all because of the smell!

Yes, I created foods and flowers to smell great, but I designed something else to smell good, too: you! Yes, you! Oh, I don't just mean you smell good after taking a bath (though you do). I love it when you give off a "sweet-smelling aroma" around your friends.

Not sure what I mean by that? Whenever you choose to respond with kindness, it smells good! When you offer a warm hello to an elderly neighbor or perform a random good deed, I smell it again. . .that lovely aroma! It doesn't take much to smell good, just treating others with the same love with which I treat you. So do your best to smell yummy, no matter who you're with.

Our lives are a Christ-like fragrance
rising up to God. But this
fragrance is perceived differently
by those who are being saved
and by those who are perishing.

2 CORINTHIANS 2:15 NLT

. . . .

Stretching Yourself

. . . .

I see you, trying to do the splits! You s-t-r-e-t-c-h those legs until you go all the way down to the floor. Ouch! Painful! If you keep working at it, your muscles will eventually stretch, and then doing the splits will be a piece of cake. The more you stretch, the more flexible you'll get.

It's the same way in your journey with Me. There are many times that I ask you to s-t-r-e-t-c-h your faith. Oh, I know. . .it hurts at first. You have trouble believing you'll make it. But if you keep on stretching your faith, before long trusting gets easier and easier.

Need an example? Remember that time you had trouble believing I would help you in your math class? You tried and tried to learn your multiplication tables. You kept stretching your faith and didn't give up, and what happened? You eventually learned how to multiply!

That's how it is when your faith is stretched. Keep trying, and before long you'll be able to move mountains!

We pray that you'll have the strength
to stick it out over the long haul—not
the grim strength of gritting your teeth
but the glory-strength God gives.
It is strength that endures the
unendurable and spills over into joy,
thanking the Father who makes us
strong enough to take part in everything
bright and beautiful that he has for us.

COLOSSIANS 1:11–12 MSG

A Mighty Fortress

· · · · · · · · · · · · · · · · · ·

Maybe you've heard the words to an old hymn called "A Mighty Fortress Is Our God." It's a song about how good I am at protecting My people and taking care of them. Think of a fortress like the forts you've played in on playgrounds. You climb up inside them and pretend to hide from your enemies. You feel safe as long as you're inside. Nothing can get to you, not even the strongest enemy!

That's how I want you to feel with Me. Safe. You are, you know. I can guard you, protect you, and keep you from harm. So many times I've done that in your life and you didn't even realize it! There have been a lot of near-miss accidents, girl!

I'm not just your fortress; I'm a *mighty* fortress. No enemy is stronger than Me. None! So stick close to Me. Stay inside the walls of My fortress, and I'll do a wonderful job protecting you.

He is my loving God and my fortress,
my stronghold and my deliverer,
my shield, in whom I take refuge,
who subdues peoples under me.

PSALM 144:2 NIV

. . . .

My Weapons

. . . .

When you hear the word *weapons*, what do you think of? Perhaps you think of a police officer wearing a gun. Or maybe you think about a solider, headed off to war. Surely the last thing you think about is yourself!

Did you know that you have weapons, too? It's true. Oh, they're not the kind you see on television or in the movies. The weapons that I've given you are found in the scripture below. I've given you the helmet of salvation. The breastplate of righteousness. The sword of the Spirit. Shoes of peace. Sounds strange, right? But here's how I want you to think of it. You're like a warrior. Every morning you wake up and put on your armor so you're protected. Put on that helmet so that you're reminded of your salvation. Put on your breastplate so that you can be covered in My righteousness and goodness. Pick up the sword of the Spirit so you can conquer any spiritual enemies. Slip on those shoes of peace so that you can remain peaceful, no matter what happens.

I care so much about you! That's why I've given you these weapons, so that you can be safe. So wear them daily. Don't forget!

So stand strong, with the belt of
truth tied around your waist and the
protection of right living on your chest.
On your feet wear the Good News of
peace to help you stand strong.
And also use the shield of faith with
which you can stop all the burning
arrows of the Evil One. Accept God's
salvation as your helmet, and take
the sword of the Spirit, which
is the word of God.

EPHESIANS 6:14–17 NCV

My Fingerprint

. . . .

Have you ever seen your own fingerprint?
It's unique, different from anyone else's.
I created yours especially for you. It's
unique—one of a kind.

I have fingerprints, too. Oh, you can't see
them with your eyes, but you can see them
in other ways. That gorgeous sunset? My
fingerprints are all over it. Those magnificent
ocean waves? My fingerprints are on those,
too!

Like yours, My fingerprints are unique,
too. The greatest artist in the world can't
paint a picture as beautiful as an evening
sky. The best chef in the world can't prepare
a meal as tasty as the sweet fruits I've
created. The most talented musician on the
planet can't create a song as beautiful as
My angel choir. All of those people have
their own fingerprints, too, and they're
lovely. . .but not as lovely as Mine.

Don't get frustrated that you're different
from others. Celebrate that unique fingerprint
and realize that I made it just for you.

I praise you because I am fearfully and wonderfully made; your works are wonderful, I know that full well.

PSALM 139:14 NIV

. . . .

Stress

. . . .

So many of My girls get stressed! When you feel stressed, it's like your stomach is tied up in knots. It's not a very fun way to live, trust Me! I wish you could relax. Take a deep breath. Give your troubles to Me.

Wondering how to do that? Here's an idea. Take a piece of paper and write down all the things that have you stressed out. Maybe you'll write something about your stresses at school. Maybe you'll add something about a broken friendship. Perhaps you'll list the ugly things that people have said to you, things that really got you upset.

After you've written down all your stresses, take the piece of paper and talk to Me about each item. You might say something like, "Lord, I give my stresses to You. Please help me with the pressures I'm facing at school." One by one you can cover the things on your list.

Then, as you reach the end, lift the paper up in the air and picture yourself placing those stresses into My hands. Then wad up the paper and toss it in the trash can. Those stresses are behind you now. They're not yours to deal with anymore. I've got this, I promise!

"Do not let your heart be
troubled; believe in God,
believe also in Me."

JOHN 14:1 NASB

. . . .

The Perfect Fit

. . . .

Remember that scene in *Cinderella* where the prince shows up with the glass slipper in his hand? He tries it on one of the wicked stepsisters, and it doesn't fit. Then he tries it on the other wicked stepsister, and it doesn't fit her, either. Finally he calls for Cinderella. She sits down and stretches out her foot, already knowing that the shoe is just her size. Sure enough! It slides right on, the perfect fit.

There's nothing better than having a perfect fit. That's what I want for you. Does this mean you have to work hard to fit in with your friends? Not at all. If the girls you're hanging out with are making you work hard to earn their friendship, then they're not the right kind of girls for you. I want you to be with friends who make it easy. Your friendships should be sweet and loving, not hard and complicated.

Somewhere out there you'll find just the right friends. They'll be the perfect fit, just like Cinderella's slipper.

All the believers were together
and had everything in common.

ACTS 2:44 NIV

. . . .

Write It on Your Heart

. . . .

Some people think that being a Christian means you have a long list of do's and don'ts. They think I'm like a judge in a courtroom, ready to bang My gavel every time they mess up. That's not true! Of course I like for My girls to play by the rules found in My Word, the Bible. But when you mess up, I don't get mad. I just show you a better way.

Here's a little secret. You can take My rules (My biblical laws) and write them on your heart. How do you do that? Don't just memorize the verse "Love others as you love yourself." Actually do it. When you write it on your heart, it just comes naturally. When it comes naturally, it's not a chore. You don't feel like it's something you have to do; it's something you get to do.

I want you to enjoy My laws. I came up with them for your protection, after all. I want you to have the best possible life. So read My Word, memorize the verses you see there, and then write them on your heart— make them a natural part of your life. What a happy life it will be!

They demonstrate that God's law is
written in their hearts, for their own
conscience and thoughts either accuse
them or tell them they are doing right.

ROMANS 2:15 NLT

. . . .

Laughter

. . . .

Did you know that laughter is a way to praise Me? It's true! When you let loose with a big belly laugh, it makes you feel so good inside. And it's a great way to celebrate the good and fun things in life. When you laugh, it's truly like medicine for your soul. Everything feels better after you've had the giggles.

Have you ever heard of a man named Job? You can find his story in My Word. What a tragic tale. Everything that could go wrong for Job did. He lost his family, his home, his health. . .everything. You wouldn't think he'd have much to laugh about, would you? So isn't it interesting that we find this scripture about laughter in the middle of Job's story? Why would a man who'd lost so much be told that I would fill his mouth with laughter?

Sweet girl, I want you to know why I made sure Job was told this: because I didn't want him to give up hope. And I don't want you to give up hope, either. You've gone through a lot of tough things, but I can promise you, there are better days ahead, days filled with laughter and joy. So brace yourself and prepare to praise through laughter. Happy days are here again.

"God will yet fill your mouth
with laughter and your lips
with shouts of joy."

JOB 8:21 NCV

. . . .

The Greatest Command

. . . .

The Bible, My Word, is divided into two sections: the Old Testament and the New Testament. The Old Testament is filled with hundreds of commands showing My people how to live. There are so many rules in the books of the Old Testament that many of My followers couldn't keep up! I'm sure many of those people wished I would trim down the list to only a few.

If you read the New Testament, you can see that I summed up all the commands into one: love Me with all of your heart and love others as you love yourself. Pause to think about that for a moment. If you really, truly loved Me with your whole heart, you would do the things I tell you to do. If you really loved others as you loved yourself, you would bend over backward to make sure people were cared for.

Why do you suppose I told My people that love is the greatest command? Why didn't I choose another one to put at the top of the list? Because all of My commandments are designed to show My children how much I love them.

" 'Love the Lord your God with all your heart and with all your soul and with all your mind and with all your strength.' The second is this: 'Love your neighbor as yourself.' There is no commandment greater than these.'

MARK 12:30–31 NIV

· ·

Pointing Fingers

. . . .

Have you ever been around people who like to point fingers? They never take the blame for anything. Instead, they always point at someone standing nearby and say, "She did it. Not me." You know they're lying because you were a witness to the truth, but you feel stuck. You don't know what to do.

I want My girls to be honest. Always. Does this mean you go around tattling on everyone? Not necessarily, but there are times when you have to tell an adult what's going on, even if it means your friend gets mad at you. It can get tricky because you don't want to turn into someone who's known for telling on others, but on the other hand, if you witness someone in a lie and they won't come clean, you have no choice but to tell the truth.

And while we're talking about this, just one more thing: there have been a few times I've seen you pointing fingers, blaming others for things you've done. That breaks My heart. The next time you get caught doing something wrong, just admit it. Tell the truth. It's always better to get things out in the open, for everyone involved!

"But in that coming day no weapon turned against you will succeed. You will silence every voice raised up to accuse you. These benefits are enjoyed by the servants of the LORD; their vindication will come from me. I, the LORD, have spoken!'

ISAIAH 54:17 NLT

Self-Esteem

. . . .

What does it mean to have self-esteem? Some would say it just means you're confident in yourself. That you're okay with yourself. I'm all about those things! I want My girls to be confident and content with who they are. But others would say that having "self"-esteem means you look to yourself for courage and confidence, and that's not true at all!

If you depend on yourself, you'll fail every time! I would rather have you depend on Me, sweet girl. I'll build you up and give you courage and confidence, I promise. You can try all day long, but "esteem" (confidence) doesn't come from staring in the mirror and saying, "You're awesome!" to your reflection. True esteem comes from knowing you are My child, created in My image, and loved no matter what.

So don't depend on yourself, okay? I have a much greater plan. Just look to Me. I'll give you everything you need. . .and more!

So God created man in his own image,
in the image of God he created him;
male and female he created them.

GENESIS 1:27 ESV

. . . .

Masterpiece

. . . .

You are a masterpiece, beautiful girl. What does this mean? A masterpiece is a "piece" (something spectacular) created by the master (Me!). If you've ever seen an expensive painting in a museum, you know it's worth a lot of money because the artist who painted it is famous. I'm the most famous Artist of all. And I took the time to craft you into My image. You're lovelier than any painting in a museum—and far more valuable!

Not only did I create you from the inside out; I breathed life into you. When you took your first breath, I was there. And when you take your last, I will be there, too. You are a masterpiece no matter what you're going through. Your body will change from year to year, but My design is perfect!

So hold your head up high! Don't let anyone tell you that you're not special, because you are! You are one of My beautiful, precious girls, and you mean more to Me than you will ever know.

Why? Because you are My masterpiece.

So God created mankind in his own image, in the image of God he created them; male and female he created them.

GENESIS 1:27 NIV

. . . .

If You Liked This Book, You'll Want to Take a Look at. . .

God Hearts Me: 3-Minute Devotions for Girls on the Go!

Written especially for girls, this devotional packs a powerful dose of comfort, encouragement, and inspiration into just-right-sized readings for young hearts. Each day's reading meets girls ages 10 to 14 right where they are—and is complemented by a relevant scripture and prayer.
Paperback / 978-1-63058-609-6 / $4.99

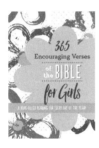

365 Encouraging Verses of the Bible for Girls

Every day for an entire year, girls will be encouraged, challenged, and inspired with great passages of scripture—addressing themes of God, Jesus, heaven, love, miracles, wisdom, and much, much more. Each devotional reading will meet girls, ages 8 to 12, right where they are—offering words of comfort, peace, and hope for everyday life.
Paperback / 978-1-68322-348-1 / $7.99